The Middle School Mind

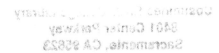

The Middle School Mind

Growing Pains in
Early Adolescent Brains

Richard M. Marshall and Sharon Neuman

ROWMAN & LITTLEFIELD EDUCATION
A division of
ROWMAN & LITTLEFIELD PUBLISHERS, INC.
Lanham • New York • Toronto • Plymouth, UK

Published by Rowman & Littlefield Education
A division of Rowman & Littlefield Publishers, Inc.
A wholly owned subsidiary of The Rowman & Littlefield Publishing Group, Inc.
4501 Forbes Boulevard, Suite 200, Lanham, Maryland 20706
http://www.rowmaneducation.com

Estover Road, Plymouth PL6 7PY, United Kingdom

British Library Cataloguing in Publication Information Available

Library of Congress Cataloging-in-Publication Data

Marshall, Richard M.
  The middle school mind : growing pains in early adolescent brains/Richard M.
Marshall and Sharon Neuman.
    p. cm.
  ISBN 978-1-61048-584-5 (cloth : alk. paper)—ISBN 978-1-61048-585-2 (pbk. : alk.
paper)—ISBN 978-1-61048-586-9 (ebook)
  1. Middle school students.   2. Middle school students—Psychology.
  3. Adolescence.   I. Neuman, Sharon   II. Title.
  HQ796.M32   2012
  305.23—dc23
                                                    2011040608

∞™ The paper used in this publication meets the minimum requirements of American
National Standard for Information Sciences—Permanence of Paper for Printed Library
Materials, ANSI/NISO Z39.48-1992.

Printed in the United States of America

Contents

Contents

Foreword

Mike Bradley, EdD

Dad sat and stared at the floor in silence. The ticking of the clock grew louder and louder as his hard eyes filled with soft tears of frustration. Finally he sighed heavily and began speaking. "I guess I'm ready now, well, to maybe listen to what you have to say—at least I'll try. But I'm not a, you know, a 'therapy' kind of guy." He used his fingers to put quotes around the word "therapy" as if it smelled bad. He raised his eyes to mine. "I have to tell you I'm kinda stunned. I just can't believe that I can't raise my kids without all this 'training' junk (more finger quotes).

"I know I'm a hard case sometimes but, I love my kids, and I'm a good person, a good parent—way, *way* better than my old man was, but—here I am. You wanna know something? In thirteen years I spanked my kid maybe twice in his life when he was small, and now at age thirteen, he calls DHS [child protective services] 'cause *I grabbed his arm? He was the one cursing at his mother! What was I supposed to do?* My kid was, like, perfect 'til thirteen and now he won't even talk except to yell at me? What in the world is going on?"

He quieted a bit. "I know lots of teenagers get a little crazy, but I always thought that was all about the weak parenting they got—you know, like if you let them get away with stuff when they're small then they go nuts when they hit middle school? I was so sure that I had this parenting gig down cold. It seemed so easy to me. I could always point out what other parents were doing wrong that made their teens go wrong. I used to point that stuff out to my wife in restaurants. And now I'm like that lousy parent getting stared at in restaurants when his kid acts out."

I suddenly recalled myself in a restaurant the night before, having dinner with my wife and thirteen-year-old daughter Sarah. As I tried to get a conversation going with Sarah by asking about her camp counselor job, she had slipped into a trance of some sort, staring away and not even acknowledging that she could hear me. Since she had recently been mysteriously ill, I was a tad worried. "Sarah," I asked, "are you OK? Sarah? Are you hearing me? Sarah?"

"DAAAAD," she exploded, "I REALLY HATE IT WHEN YOU GO 'PSY-CHOLOGY' ON ME! JUST—STOP—TALKING, *OOOOKAAAAYYY?*" She wagged her head and rolled her eyes in perfect timing with the sarcastic "*OOOOKAAAAYYY*" which was also perfectly timed for all of the now-turning heads in the restaurant, watching to see how I would respond.

There I sat—a thirty-five year therapist, a best-selling author of four parenting books, a TV parenting expert and an international lecturer on parenting—with my cheeks turning red, and my right hand mystically prompted by my Irish Catholic ancestors to slap Sarah's face. In the name of good parenting, of course.

Parenting can look so easy, even as it did over three hundred years ago to an author named John Wilmot. Easy, that is, until he had kids. "Before I got married," he wrote, "I had six theories about bringing up children; now I have six children, and no theories." I love that quote. It helps me to be more accepting of my own uncertainties about parenting my own children, which to this day can put a knot in my stomach. But over the years I have found "antacids" for my "parenting heartburn," the latest being this excellent book you now hold in your hands.

Sharon and Richard (your authors) have put together a masterful work which calmly and plainly explains the chaos and complexity now confronting you as an intervener (parent, counselor, teacher and so on) with an early teen. First, they offer the cutting-edge science that expands our knowledge of how teen brains work, and more importantly, of how they often *don't* work. Acquiring knowledge is the first step of competency, the foundation of intervention skill.

But the genius I see in their book are more the stories, the fly-on-the-wall insights into early teen behavior, and even more importantly, into early teen experience. It is that gift of learning about teen experience, of "what it's like to be thirteen these days," that builds the framing of the most critical intervention skill, a thing called *empathy*. Empathy is a tool that doesn't ask *if* what kids say makes sense to us, but instead seeks to understand *how* what kids say makes sense *to them*. Without that intervention skill, not much good can happen.

That other night in the restaurant, knowledge helped me understand why my daughter exploded at me as she did, and that was a great help. But it was rather the *empathy* that kept my hand away from her face. Understanding how tough it is to be thirteen in today's world provides a compassion that calms angry learned reflexes, be they Irish Catholic or otherwise. "I'm sorry I made you feel bad, Sarah," I calmly responded. "Let me know if you'd like to chat later. I love hearing about your world."

On that night, knowledge and empathy won the day, as they have on so many days before, and as they hopefully will for the remainder of my parenting tour of duty. It is my wish that those very precious gifts that you'll find in this book may help you, even as they have saved me.

Good luck out there.

Dr. Mike Bradley, an internationally recognized psychologist, author, and expert on adolescent behavior, has appeared on hundreds of TV and radio shows, received ten national publishing awards, and is also the recipient of a William Penn Humanitarian Award, Commission on Human Relations.

Acknowledgements

First, we would like to thank our spouses and children for their support in allowing us to take the time to work together on this project. Without their encouragement, this book would not have been possible. Their support throughout this project has been invaluable.

We also appreciate the time that our friends gave to review a copy of the manuscript and give us their feedback. A big thank you goes to Phil Allen, Michelle DiGioia, Dr. Richard Frates, Susie Kallan, David Lewis, Dr. Sherrie Nickell, Lisa Rosa, and Punam V. Saxena. Their input was invaluable.

Thank you to Dr. Mike Bradley, author of *Yes, Your Teen is Crazy*, for agreeing to write the foreword for us. We are honored to have him participate in this project and to share his thoughts with our readers.

We cannot express enough gratitude to Tom Koerner, our publishing editor, who gave us a chance at a dream of publishing a book about middle school youth. If it wasn't for Dr. Jerry Valentine, who also believed in us, we would not have been able to share our thoughts in print. A big thank you goes to Tom Koerner and Jerry Valentine! Thanks for believing in us and giving us a chance to share how great middle schoolers really are.

Chapter 1

Middle School for Middle Schoolers

So what is it with middle school students? In the year prior to starting middle school, parents clearly recall that their son or daughter was a cooperative youngster, sailing through elementary school like an old pro, enthusiastic about a range of hobbies and interests, and hanging out (texting) with a collection of same-sex friends. Sure, there were some minor disappointments, but—by and large—elementary school was a happy time at home and in school. So what happened in the summer between fifth and sixth grade? And what is this thing called middle school?

If you have raised or are now raising a child in middle school, you know that whatever happened didn't just happen in the summer. As in all of life's changes, the transition from childhood to adulthood is a gradual process. It's not as though our children cross some mythical river that changes them from shiny-faced cherubs into some foreign species. Oh, maybe some other kids change and maybe some of our kids' friends begin moving in the wrong directions. But not ours. Our children may be influenced by others, but we raised ours right and we don't have "those problems."

But things sure are different in middle school. Parents are shocked to learn that in middle school, children as young as twelve or thirteen are sexually active—very sexually active. And that girls use foul language—real foul language. And that kids can now purchase (or, in some case, be given) drugs while at school. And that some girls wear different colors of bracelets that indicate what sex acts they are willing to perform with what gender.

Parents struggle to grasp the enormity of this change. They search for an explanation, some way of understanding how their child is ever going to cope with this torrent of drugs, physical intimidation, openly sexual activity, and—oh yes, lest we forget—stiffer academic challenges, choosing electives,

1

more homework, and less support from teachers who now are responsible for one hundred and fifty students instead of a single class of twenty-four as it was in elementary school.

Parents look at their child's elementary school and then they look at the middle school and they are in shocked disbelief. They wonder aloud, "How in the world did anyone decide that putting hundreds of same age, different sex, newly minted teenagers in one place would be a good idea?"

Well, to answer that question, we have to go back to 1888. In that year, Charles Eliot, the president of Harvard, and other professional educators on the National Education Association's Committee of Ten on Secondary School Studies concluded that students in grades seven and eight were wasting their time in school. At the time, there were two levels of schooling in the United States: elementary school and high school.

All students were encouraged to attend elementary school for grades kindergarten through eight. Those interested in going to college then took an entrance exam to be admitted to high school. At the time, high schools offered a college preparatory curriculum to a small number of students (about 5–6 percent) who were planning to go on to college.

Eliot and the other members of the Committee of Ten were increasingly concerned about the large number of students who dropped out of school after the sixth grade; it would be 1918 before all states had compulsory education laws. And second, the Committee was looking for a way to encourage talented students to go on to high school. Their solution was to move grades seven and eight to the high school and to end elementary school at grade six.

By 1920, most states had adopted the idea of an introductory experience that they named "junior high school." It spanned grades seven through nine. By 1960, 80 percent of young adolescents were attending a junior high school.[1]

But things didn't end there. By the 1960s, educators acknowledged that junior high schools were not meeting the unique needs of students in this transition zone between elementary school and high school. In the first place, ninth graders had to pass their courses successfully in order to earn the Carnegie units needed for high school graduation. Consequently, in 1965, William Alexander and Emmett Williams recommended that ninth grade be returned to high school and that grades six through eight comprise what they called the "middle school," specifically designed to meet the needs of student in grades six through eight.

A year later, Donald Eichorn published the first book detailing the educational and social principles of the middle school experience. Among his recommendations were the elimination of highly competitive activities (e.g., interscholastic sports and prom queen contests) in favor of activities that provided all students an opportunity to participate (e.g., intramural sports). He also called for a greater range of activities that students could use to explore and develop interests and abilities that were just emerging in this age group.

By the middle 1970s the National Middle School Association had been formed, reflecting the growing acceptance of the idea that grades six through eight comprised middle school. Still, by the late 1980s, it was becoming clear that the new middle schools were much different than the old junior high schools.

Moreover, there was a growing body of middle school research revealing a decline in motivation and academic achievement among students just entering middle school. To make matters worse, there was a grudging admission that middle schools were not meeting the unique social and emotional needs characteristic of early adolescents.

More than a hundred years ago, educators realized that youngsters just entering adolescence had unique needs that were not being met with existing educational programs and policies. Though it is safe to assume that the country's ten thousand or so middle schools are better at meeting these needs now than they were a hundred (or even ten) years ago, the middle school reform movement is far from over. Despite all the improvements, despite all the parent advice columns, and all the teacher workshops and principal trainings, middle school children continue to test the patience, the endurance, and the stamina of parents and teachers alike.

As you can see, even from this brief discussion, early adolescents have posed a challenge for educators since public schools were first established. For more than a century, educators have struggled to decide where elementary school ends and high school begins. What we have learned is that early adolescents have unique needs. They have outgrown the need for the nurturing that they received from their elementary school teachers, but they are not quite ready for the academic demands or the social challenges of high school.

Chapter 2

Middle Schoolers:
Ages Twelve to Fourteen

WHAT'S A MIDDLE SCHOOLER?

Despite all the academic debates about how to structure middle schools, what to teach, how to teach it, when to teach it, there is one constant: the middle school student. Who is this person? What is it about middle schoolers that has prompted professional educators to struggle for over a hundred years to create a special place for this age group? Are they really so unique that they need a special place with a special curriculum for two or three years?

To help us understand the children who occupy the transition zone between childhood and adulthood, let's begin with what is known about this age group. First, they are just entering the developmental stage called adolescence. If you look up "adolescence" in the *Encyclopedia of Children's Health*, you will find this definition:

> The word adolescence is Latin in origin, derived from the verb *adolescere,* which means "to grow into adulthood." Adolescence is a time of moving from the immaturity of childhood into the maturity of adulthood. There is no single event or boundary line that denotes the end of childhood or the beginning of adolescence. Rather, experts think of the passage from childhood into and through adolescence as composed of a set of transitions that unfold gradually and that touch upon many aspects of the individual's behavior, development, and relationships. These transitions are biological, cognitive, social, and emotional.[2]

This definition reminds us that there is "no single event or boundary that denotes the end of childhood or the beginning of adolescence"; that adolescence is a "set of transitions that unfold gradually"; and that it touches upon "many aspects of the individual's behavior, development, and relationships."

Except for the rapid period of maturation and growth that occurs between birth and the start of kindergarten, no other phase of a person's life comes close to matching the changes that occur during adolescence. Except for some vague memories of the "terrible twos," most parents generally view their children's early years with amazement as they watch them transition from helpless infants to independent kindergarteners ready to take on the challenges of school and life.

Unlike early childhood, however, the adolescent years are far more difficult for children and parents. Why that is and what parents can do about it begins with an understanding of what it must be like to be an adolescent. Let's consider two components of the definition.

NO SINGLE EVENT OR BOUNDARY

The gradual unfolding referred to in the definition begins at about age twelve and ends sometime after age twenty. Although adolescence coincides with puberty, some children reach their adolescent years prior to puberty, while others start puberty prior to age twelve. The ability to reproduce represents a convenient starting point, though it is important to remember that at age fourteen some boys and girls have not reached puberty (a biological event) even though they are experiencing the cognitive, social, and emotional changes associated with adolescence. Think of it as "early adolescence lite."

A more compelling reason for using puberty as the start of adolescence has to do with changes in brain chemistry that occur at this time. The onset of puberty results in the production and release of hormones that will, over the next few years, alter children's height, weight, body shape, and, perhaps more importantly, drive them to seek independence from the primary caretakers.

If you wonder why young teens act "crazy," consider this. Imagine that at age forty, you suddenly went through something comparable to adolescence. In addition to being reminded that you are, indeed, middle-aged, your body suddenly and unexpectedly starts to change. Body parts grow bigger, you get heavier (even though your eating hasn't changed) and taller. In a matter of months, you have outgrown all the clothes in your closet.

If you are a woman, you notice that men are looking at you differently and they are making comments about your body. If you are a man, and you are experiencing what an adolescent experiences, you notice that you have more energy, you are seeking adventure, but you also want to sleep until early afternoon. And even though you are happily married and have young children, you have heightened sexual desires that you find difficult to control. You try to change, to go back to who you are (were), but nothing works. You have lost control of your body. Whatever has overtaken you, you are unable to do anything about it. You feel helpless, out of control, and scared.

Moreover if these physical changes are not enough, imagine that you no longer have control over your emotions. Feelings come and go for no apparent reason. You are happy one moment and sad the next. You are experiencing more feelings and they are more intense. You are sure that everyone is watching you, that they notice every flaw, that they are critical of how you look and how you act. You have lost your confidence and you are not sure how to get it back. Should you try to fit in or go your separate way?

Imagine how difficult it would be if your body suddenly and unexpectedly began to change and you began to experience new, intense, and overwhelming emotions. Think of how it would feel if you were sure that everyone was staring at you and that they were criticizing you behind your back. Would you be able to concentrate at work? Would you be able to make plans for the future? Would you be able to keep your life neatly organized? As a forty-year-old, you know how it ends. Early adolescents have no idea where this is going or how it is going to end.

A SET OF TRANSITIONS

In addition to loss of control, another unique feature about early adolescence that makes it so difficult is not just the kinds of changes that occur during this developmental period, but the magnitude of the changes that occur. There are huge differences between a twelve-year-old and a twenty-year-old. A twelve-year-old boy is finishing his last season of Little League baseball. Dwight Gooden was a starting pitcher for the New York Mets when he was nineteen.

Along with increased size, strength, and coordination, there are also significant changes in children's thinking abilities, in their moral development, in their emotional development, and in their social interactions. These changes do not come easily, however. And therein, as they say, is the rub. Changing from a child to an adult comes at a price. In a way, adolescence is a sort of slow-motion version of *The Incredible Hulk*.

From 1978 to 1982, *The Incredible Hulk* was a popular TV series. For those who missed this series and the 2008 movie version, the main character (Dr. Bruce Banner) was the subject of a gamma radiation experiment that went horribly wrong. Now, when events cause his heart rate to accelerate, he transforms into a green-skinned hulk with superhuman strength that, thanks to his pre-experiment personality, he uses in benevolent ways.

Though the effects are positive, each transformation from human to hulk is a painfully wrenching process. In the Hulk's case, however, the transformation takes less than a minute and the pain subsides. For teenagers, the transformation takes years.

In the appendix there is a long list of over fifty characteristics that describe the middle school student. Just a quick glance helps adults appreciate just how complex the transition from childhood to adulthood really is. Glancing through the many websites and magazine articles that promise to help parents help their child prepare for middle school can produce a small chuckle. Typically, these sites offer parents eight to ten practical suggestions. Though these suggestions may be helpful, they address only a tiny fraction of the issues that our middle school students are about to encounter.

WHAT IS IT LIKE TO BE AN EARLY ADOLESCENT?

To be an adolescent is to be at least two (sometimes more than two) people. One is the child who still depends on parents for money, rides, school supplies, food, clean laundry, and keeping her safe at night. The other is the emerging adult she is trying desperately to become. This emerging adult, by the way, believes that she should be more independent than her parents allow; that she is smarter than you; that she is already better at some things than you are; and that she can handle the risks that are out there.

Raising these two people at the same time can be demanding. There are really only three child-rearing choices for parents and teachers who are responsible for early adolescents. Choice one is for adults to make all the decisions about grades, curfews, dating, selection of friends, selection of activities, chores, and so on. This child-rearing style is known as authoritarian parenting, in which the parent is "the decider" and the child must conform to the parent's wishes "or else." "Or else," one can only suspect, means "or else the child is going to be punished for not conforming."

Choice two is for adults to give up and "let the kids raise themselves." The thinking here is that one can't do much about it anyway, so just let them go and hope they survive and turn out all right. This is known as *laissez-faire* parenting. *Laissez-faire* is a French term that means let it be; what will happen will happen. Despite what they may think, early adolescents are not ready to raise themselves. The adult world they encounter after elementary school is filled with dangers about which they know little. Of course, they will argue that they can "handle it," and though they may want to begin making their own decisions, they are not really ready to do so on their own.

The third choice is for parents and teens to work together. Because parents are the mature side of this equation, it falls to them to try to understand what it must be like to be an early adolescent in transition. What is it like to be about twelve, thirteen, or fourteen and having a body that is out of control, having emotions that are out of control, trying desperately to fit in somewhere, and being judged (usually very harshly) every day by parents, teachers, and peers?

Many adults argue that choice one (parent in charge) is the only option. The thinking goes something like: kids need to know that adults make the rules, and if they don't obey they will suffer the consequences. The intervention of choice is punishment, especially if the child breaks a rule or falls short of parental expectations.

Choice two, as anyone who has raised a teenager knows, is an invitation for disaster. Early adolescents are simply not ready to raise themselves, despite what they think and despite how they argue to the contrary. As difficult as it sometimes is to raise (or to teach) a teenager, adults must persist. Parents must hang in there. Turn youngsters loose and a parent's worst nightmares will likely come true.

Choice three is one in which the child and the adult begin to make rules together and to solve problems (including settling differences) by introducing the child to the concept of negotiated settlement. Ross Greene, an associate professor in the Department of Psychiatry at Harvard Medical School, developed a program that he calls Collaborative Problem Solving. Like it or not, puberty ushers in a period of transition that is going to change our docile, obedient, and adoring child. And like it or not, these changes are going to redefine your relationship.

Choice three is based on three core beliefs. First, most children (including teens) do what they are supposed to do most of the time. Second, children need not be rewarded for things they are supposed to do. And third, adults should teach, and be prepared to reteach, children how to do things, rather than punish them for not doing so. Hopefully, adults will opt for choice three.

When teachers are asked what qualities they want their students to possess, they invariably respond that they want them to be self-motivated, independent, and in control of their own behavior, even when adults are not present. Choice one, authoritarian parenting, does just the opposite. It tells the child that adults make the rules, that adults don't trust them, that adults are constantly watching them, and that adults will punish them if they make a mistake.

Choice two actually denies children the opportunity to learn self-regulation and self-motivation. The *laissez-faire* approach leaves children without direction, without goals, without a destination, and without a standard to measure themselves. This is a recipe for trouble.

Choice three is the only approach that gives teens the opportunity to learn how to make decisions, how to set and maintain boundaries, and how to negotiate with others. Of course, they will make some mistakes, but the mistakes they make belong to them as well as to you. They are far less likely to blame others when they have been part of the process. Moreover, it is far better to make mistakes while they still have their parents' safety net to protect them from really serious trouble.

Collaboration is not easy. It is difficult for adults and children to change old habits. Throughout elementary school, children grew accustomed to receiving orders and following them. Once they get to middle school, however, they are ready to take on more decision-making responsibility. Generally speaking, teenagers want more control and more decision making than teachers or parents are ready to give them.

Youngsters have to learn that there are limits, but learning this is not easy for adults or for teens. Lots of battles may ensue, but it is okay. Minor skirmishes are part of the process. Just as our children grew accustomed to taking orders, parents and teachers grew accustomed to giving them. It won't be easy deciding how much of that authority you are willing and able to give up, but give you must.

Once parents (and teachers) have made that difficult decision, there is one more thing to do. They need to understand what it's like to be an early adolescent. If you are going to be effective in this collaborative effort, you will need to understand your partner. Remember that wonderful observation about Ginger Rogers—she did everything Fred Astaire did, but backwards and in high heels. Well, think of yourself as Ginger Rogers.

Or think of it this way: If you were making a speech to a group of twenty fighter pilots, would you lecture them—or even worse—would you try to lead them into combat? Not likely; unless you have been one, you don't have the foggiest notion of what it is like to be in aerial combat. It's the same with teens; you can't (or you shouldn't) talk about what you don't know. Try to, and you lose your audience.

Of course, you were a teenager once, but that doesn't qualify you to lead your teen into combat. You are from a different era, and you are not your child. You know what your teenage experience was like. You can only observe and assume what your children's teenage experiences are like. You know that feeling that comes over you when your children tell you that you don't understand; that things are different now than when you are growing up? Well, they're right. Don't tell them, but they're right. Because no matter how young (hip, with it, current) you think you are, you are and will remain obsolete.

Their life experience is vastly different from yours, and though you may understand parts of their world, there are parts of it that you just can't know. Though you argue that you have gone through what they are going through, you never did and you aren't going to. What kind of a computer were you using when you were thirteen? And what was available on the Internet? Better yet, was there an Internet? What were the video games like when you were thirteen? You can now receive 1,363 channels through a cable TV provider. How many choices did you have when you were that age?

When you were their age, you did not have Facebook and other social networking sites that have changed the early adolescent experience in ways that we cannot possibly understand. Let's face it, children are growing up in a different world. And there are parts of it that you don't (and won't) understand.

Okay, so you don't know how to play *Call of Duty*. And you have never experienced the relational aggression of Facebook. But there are some things that you do share with your young adolescents. The first is a brain. Yes, despite opinion to the contrary, everyone has one. And at some time after age ten or eleven, the human brain reaches puberty and everything changes. This change is so dramatic, so life-changing, that the passage from childhood to adulthood is embedded in almost all cultures and in religious customs that have existed for thousands of years.

In the Jewish tradition, the transition to adulthood is marked with the *bar mitzvah*. In Islam it is known as *mukallaf,* and like its Jewish brother it means that the young adult is ready to bear the responsibility of God's law. In various Christian traditions, children assume the same responsibility with the rite of confirmation. The key word here is responsibility.

Despite its religious and cultural significance, the transition to adulthood is foremost a biological event. For both boys and girls, puberty is the point at which they can reproduce. It just so happens that reproductive capacity entails a host of other brain changes that result in major changes in the way one looks, how one thinks, and how one feels.

The comedian, Bill Cosby, once referred to teens as being brain-damaged; more recently, Michael Bradley, a therapist, wrote a book entitled *Yes, Your Teen is Crazy*. Though each overstates the case, these fathers capture accurately the fact that, whatever else is set off with puberty, the biggest change occurs north of one's shoulders. Damaged? No; Crazy? Possibly.

But damaged and crazy don't tell much about the teen brain nor what to do about your teenager's sometimes zany, sometimes scary behaviors. For that, you need a more accurate description of what it is going on "up there." Because what is going on "up there" is far more important than what is going on "down there."

Middle school students have gotten a bad rap. There is a perception, even among many educators, that middle school students are impossibly difficult to deal with and that middle schools are best avoided. This is an unfortunate misconception. Early adolescents are not evil; they are struggling through the difficult transition from childhood to adulthood.

Much of what adults consider misbehavior is actually the child's effort to manage this transition. They do the best they can with the resources they have, but their resources are often inadequate. That's where adults fit in. Even though young teens argue that they can do it themselves, they really do need us. But this relationship has to be a collaborative one. We need to work with them, not just impose our will on them. Rather than simply enforcing rules on them, our most important job as parents and teachers is to help children develop self-regulation and self-motivation, because these are the crucial skills they will need in adulthood.

Chapter 3

Adolescent Brains

The brain is unlike any other organ in the body. If you put your fists together so that your knuckles and the bottoms of your palms are touching, you'll have an idea of how big your brain is. The adult brain weighs about three pounds. It is divided into two halves called hemispheres that are joined together by a thick band of white connecting fibers called the corpus callosum. This band of fibers allows the two halves of the brain to communicate with each other.

When most of us think of the brain, we think of a wrinkled clump of firm tissue. But this is not an accurate picture of what the brain really looks like and how it works. To begin with, we have five brains, not one. That wrinkled part that we see in pictures is the fifth of the five brains. It is called the cortex, which means bark. And like the bark of a tree, it is just a thin covering.

The cortex is only three millimeters thick, about the diameter of a pencil eraser. But this may be the most important three millimeters in our body, because the cortex contains six layers of neurons that produce movement, receive sensory information from our bodies, produce our thoughts, and inhibit our emotions.

In the brain's frontal areas, we find the cells that are responsible for planning, organizing, abstract thinking, short-term memory, and selective attention. In the back half of the brain are the neurons that register incoming sensory information. In fact, all sensory information enters the back half of the brain and gradually moves to the front of the brain where the frontal lobes decide what to do about it. For example, if the back half of the brain sees a car coming toward you, the front half of the brain sees to it that you move out of the way.

In addition to all of these functions, we use the neurons in the front of the cortex to control or inhibit our emotions. But, as luck would have it, the

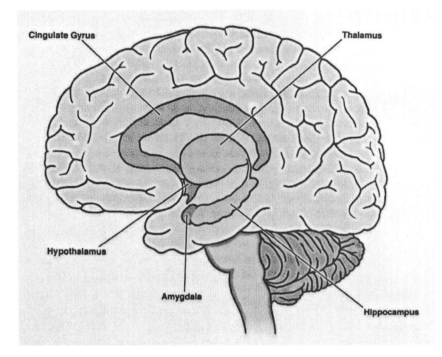

Figure 3.1.

frontal lobe is the last part of the brain to mature. Therefore, whatever emotions teens produce, the ability to inhibit those emotions is at a distinct disadvantage, because the neurons that do the inhibiting are simply not mature enough to compete with their much more intense emotional cousins.

But even as adults, we experience this conflict between arousal and inhibition. Road rage is an example. What happens in road rage? Too much arousal, too little inhibition. And if emotions can occasionally overwhelm adults who have mature frontal lobes, imagine how quickly and how often emotions can overwhelm early adolescents who do not yet have the capacity for inhibition.

When you think of it, all of our emotions are really just responses to incoming sensory information from environmental events or from thoughts that we conjure. The structures that produce these emotions and that respond to events in our environment are located in our second brain, the limbic system. Limbus means ring, and as the name implies, the limbic system is a circle of seven structures that first receive and then respond to sensory events that occur around us. The picture above shows the location of each structure.

Each of these structures has one or more jobs to do. To understand how these structures work, it is helpful to begin with the thalamus. This egg-shaped structure consists of about twenty different clusters of neurons. Each cluster takes sensory input from one of our senses and then transmits that information to the area of the cortex that receives that input. For example, electrical inputs from the retina travel to an area of the thalamus called the lateral geniculate nucleus. Lateral means that this area is on the side; geniculate means that it is shaped like a knee, and nucleus means that it is a cluster of neurons.

The lateral geniculate nucleus, in turn, transmits the electrical current to the primary visual cortex in the back of the cortex. The primary visual cortex is where vision occurs. That's where we "see" and recognize objects and words. Once we recognize the object, the electrical current travels to the front of the brain. On its way, the sensory information passes through the limbic system. If the limbic system remembers that this object is a threat (say a poisonous snake) the limbic structures will prepare you to take appropriate action. If the fear is sufficiently threatening, it will cause your amygdala to initiate the fight-or-flight response.

Another limbic structure, the hypothalamus, regulates our survival mechanisms. Its job is to ensure the survival of the individual (by regulating food and fluid intake and by controlling other mechanisms like body temperature and sleep) and the survival of the species (through reproductive activities). Years ago, a comedian became famous for the line, "The devil made me do it." He was on the right track. Actually, his hypothalamus made him do it.

The hypothalamus motivates us to do what we need to do to keep ourselves and our species alive and well. It is the hypothalamus that tells us when we are thirsty and moves us to get something to drink. When your room gets too cold, your hypothalamus responds by making you shiver and sneeze (both of which make you move and warm your body). Once you are warm enough, the hypothalamus tells your body to stop moving.

Because it is important for us to remember what is dangerous, the limbic system also contains structures that make new memories. We have all touched a hot stove at least once, but once was enough. We never did it again, because our hippocampus made a permanent memory of that episode.

The limbic system also produces our aggressive tendencies. When sufficiently stimulated, our amygdala will react by sending us into fight or flight. Most of the time, we are able to control our emotions, but if pushed far enough, we can "lose it" and resort to more primitive (aggressive) behaviors. When angered, we are fully capable of lashing out at others. When we watch a sad movie we can be moved to tears. In this case, our ability to inhibit our crying is overwhelmed by our feelings.

THE ADOLESCENT PARADOX

At a symposium on the adolescent brain, a leading physician challenged participants with two questions: 1. Why is it that despite a rapid increase in strength, coordination, and good health, there is a 200 percent increase in mortality and morbidity among adolescents? And 2. Despite increased mental abilities, why do adolescents display more emotionally influenced behavior than children or adults?[3]

Though we are all capable of letting our emotions get the better of us, teenagers are especially vulnerable. The reason is simple. With the onset of puberty, their brains begin to produce and release new chemicals, including steroid hormones. If you have ever seen a holiday fireworks display, you'll have a fair picture of what is involved. You know, that part at the end when they send off a bunch of fireworks all at once. That is kind of what a teenager's brain is like. Lots of bright lights and lots of loud sounds. And, like the fireworks, you can never be sure when the next one is coming.

These new brain chemicals produce a range of new emotions and they intensify existing ones. What were once petty jealousies suddenly become intense rivalries. What were once tendencies become obsessions. During elementary school, we watched with amusement as our children encountered their first episodes of "puppy love." In middle school, we watch in horror when they find their "soul mate," and they tell us that they are prepared to give up everything to be together forever. Or the person your daughter has been communicating with via the Internet suddenly turns up at school to meet her in person.

This chemical tsunami is doubly difficult for newly minted adolescents. To begin with, their frontal lobes (those areas that contain the neurons that we use to inhibit our emotions) are not mature enough to do much inhibiting. As a result, emotions get to do pretty much as they please. Over the next five to six years, the frontal lobes will continue to mature. Each year they will get better at inhibiting, but for most early adolescents, emotions reign supreme.

In addition to the effects of frontal lobe maturation, parents and teachers will use these same five or six years to assist students in learning how to manage their emotions. By late adolescence, students have had five to six years of training and experience in coping with their emotional up and downs. At ages twelve or thirteen, however, they have had little or no experience with the changes that are occurring. So, in addition to less inhibition, early adolescents have fewer skills and strategies to deal with their newly discovered emotions.

HOLD ON A MINUTE

At this point you are probably thinking, wait a minute—not all teens are like this. In fact, some seem perfectly capable of having normal family relations, doing well in school, and managing the new emotions they are experiencing. And, of course, you would be correct. Not all teens are derailed by puberty; many seem to manage middle school just fine. Children with an easy temperament tend to be adolescents with an easy temperament; they seem to be more accepting and more resilient. Children with loving, supportive, and understanding parents also tend to do better.

In fact, the overwhelming majority of teens, something like 80 percent, get through this difficult period without running away, without hurting themselves, without serious accidents, and without alienating most of humanity. It's not a smooth, uneventful journey, but most teens (and parents) survive the experience without permanent damage.

But while it is true that only about 20 percent of adolescents are derailed during this period, all of them are affected to some extent by poor impulse control and by an increased urge to engage in risk-taking and sensation-seeking behaviors. And while most teens survive adolescence more or less intact, they are different at journey's end than they were when they started. And these changes are not limited to teens in modern American culture.

In 1991, two researchers studied 187 cultures around the world. Virtually all had some ritual marking the end of childhood and they all ended with the assumption of adult roles. But why this? And why now? Because they have a brain.

Until about twenty years ago, it was generally believed that human brain development was completed by about age ten and that the brain reached full maturity around the time of puberty. We now know that the teenage brain is not, as one Harvard epilepsy specialist aptly put it, "just an adult brain with fewer miles on it."[4] It is, rather, a brain on its way to adulthood. And there are numerous changes that are going to occur between puberty and age thirty.

While there is no easy explanation for the many brain changes that occur during adolescence, it is useful to begin with two organizing principles. The first is that with puberty, the brain releases hormones that result in the ability to reproduce, the development of secondary sex characteristics, and the urge to engage in risky activities. And second, because the frontal lobes of the brain are not fully developed until we are in our mid- to late twenties, they are unable to inhibit the intense emotions that appear at this time.

Throughout the last century, it was generally believed that adolescence could be explained as a contest between raging hormones and lack of impulse control. This was the notion that prompted G. Stanley Hall, one of American's first child psychologists, to label adolescence as a time of storm and stress. Since then, however, we have learned that there is much more going on in the adolescent brain than hormones and self-control. Here is a partial list of some of the brain changes that occur:

Pruning: There is a surge of synaptic growth during early adolescence. This overgrowth interferes with learning. By late adolescence, pruning reduces synaptic connections, making the ones that remain operate more efficiently. The neural networks that remain will be the ones that teens will use as adults. Pruning also does away with circuits that once were in place but were never used. This explains why young children can learn a second language with little effort and speak it without an accent. After puberty, learning a second language takes intense study, and we speak with an accent.

Frontal lobes: By late adolecence, the frontal lobes will be better able to manage risk taking and poor impulse control. Until then, parents and teachers are advised to exercise extreme caution and persistence.

Dopamine: Dopamine release makes us feel better. Unfortunately, dopamine isn't in full production, so teens seek activities that are associated with increased dopamine stimulation. High-risk behaviors and new adventures cause a release of dopamine. Go figure.

Melatonin: Melatonin helps us go to sleep. Levels of this neurotransmitter rise later in the day for teens than for preteens and adults. This explains why teenagers stay up later and why 20 percent of high schoolers fall asleep in the first two hours of school. After two school districts in Minnesota started high school one hour later, there was a significant reduction in drop outs and depression.

Amygdala and hippocampus changes: The amygdala (perceives what is dangerous) and the hippocampus (remembers what is dangerous) respond more intensely during adolescence. It's not just raging hormones; adolescent brain parts work differently.

GABA receptors: GABA receptors increase during puberty. We know that GABA receptors interfere with learning in mice. They probably do the same in humans, as the memory systems are comparable.

The best explanation of why adolescents act the way they do has to do with the status of their brains. With the onset of puberty, the brain's emotional structures are sent into high gear. Unfortunately, the parts of the brain that inhibit these emotions have not yet fully matured. Hence, we have the familiar teenage pattern of too much emotion and too little inhibition. In addition to explaining the dramatic increase in mortality and morbidity in this otherwise healthy population, this excitatory/inhibitory differential also explains why teens put off their science fair project until the night before it is due.

By early adulthood, the brain will mature and stabilize. But in the meantime, parents and teachers need to appreciate that teenagers' brains are going through profound changes. This awareness makes it easier to understand and appreciate Mark Twain's recommendation that we put teenagers in a barrel at age twelve and seal the bunghole when they are sixteen. We need to make sure, however, that we don't try to reduce all that teenagers experience to neurobiology. If it were just a matter of biology, the teen experience would probably look pretty much the same from person to person.

There are vast differences in how individuals manage during their teen years and in how they turn out as adults. Despite sharing the same DNA, even identical twins will differ in some respects. These differences suggest that other environmental factors are at work. And it is with these other factors that parents and teachers are able to exert their influence.

Chapter 4

Identity Formation

As we have already noted, puberty is essentially a biological event. At some time between ages ten and fifteen, boys and girls begin to produce brain chemicals that result in secondary sex characteristics and the ability to reproduce. Whereas puberty manifests as physical and chemical changes, adolescence is generally associated with psychological and social changes. Adolescence is a developmental phase during which children transition from childhood to adulthood.

We often think of puberty as the onset of adolescence as there is some obvious overlap, but some children reach puberty by age ten while others don't until age fifteen. Whereas puberty lasts about two years, adolescence is generally thought to begin at about age twelve or thirteen and extend into the mid-twenties.

To appreciate fully the profound changes associated with adolescence, it is helpful to stand on the shoulder of two giants—Sigmund Freud and Erik Erikson—who were some of the first to explain that human development occurs in stages. Although the focus of much criticism and the brunt of many jokes, it was Freud (1856–1939) who taught us that children are different from adults.

Prior to Freud, it was generally assumed that children were simply little adults, and it was expected that they would think and act in adult-like ways. Those who did not were considered defiant (and needed to be punished) or possessed by demons (and needed to be punished). Did you ever wonder where the phrase, "beat the devil out of him" came from? There was little understanding of (and even less tolerance for) nonconforming children, and they were dealt with firmly and decisively.

In a very real sense, Freud is the first child psychologist. That children develop in stages, that they acquire increasingly more complex abilities at each stage of development, shows that they think differently and see the world differently than adults. Freud also explained that the struggle to become more competent and to develop new abilities is sometimes a difficult one.

Freud believed that a child's personality was fully developed by age five. For that reason, his stage theory was confined mainly to developmental changes that occurred prior to puberty. In fact, it was Freud who named the period from ages nine to twelve the latency stage, implying that nothing much of importance happened during these years of relative quiet.

It was one of Freud's students, a young artist by the name of Erik Erikson (1902–1994), who provided a more complete explanation of human development. Erikson was born in Denmark. His birth father refused to marry his mother, but he was later adopted by his mother's husband, a pediatrician. The young (and headstrong) Erikson didn't like the atmosphere of formal classrooms, and rather than following in his stepfather's footsteps, he decided to study art.

One of his first jobs was to give art lessons to the children of Americans who came to study in Freud's Psychoanalytic Institute. It was Freud's daughter, Anna, who convinced him to enter the Institute. Though he lacked a college degree and any professional training, his writings gained the attention of both mentors and colleagues and he soon became a valued member of the Institute.

Erikson moved to the United States in 1933 and became one of this country's first child analysts. For the next sixty years he held positions at some of our country's most prestigious institutions, including Harvard, Berkeley, Yale, and the Menninger Foundation. He also traveled extensively, studying children from various countries and various ages, some with developmental disabilities and psychological disorders.

Unlike Freud, Erikson believed that we continue to develop across the life span. He identified eight stages of psychosocial development, beginning with infancy and proceeding through late adulthood. A crucial aspect of Erikson's theory is that in each stage of development there is a conflict between two opposing urges, one that leads to increased developmental competence and one that delays or forestalls development.

If the person is successful in resolving this conflict, he or she is prepared for the next stage of development. If the struggle is unresolved, maturational processes are delayed, and the person enters the next stage with unresolved issues that can interfere with the resolution of conflicts at subsequent stages of development.

For example, during the second stage of development (roughly ages two and three) young children begin to separate from their parents and to develop an individual identity distinct from their primary caregiver. This is the time when children begin to say "no" and to struggle for control over who decides what goes into their bodies (this is the beginning of food preferences) and what comes out of the their bodies (potty training).

When parents allow their children to exercise even a small degree of control, children more readily develop a sense of "I can do this myself," allowing them to develop what Erikson called *autonomy*. This awareness of being a separate person is a necessary stage in a person's development. But like most developmental transitions, this is not an easy one for parents or children, and it is easy to understand why parents sometimes mistakenly interpret this normal drive for competence and independence as disobedience and defiance.

Once parents label their child's newly discovered drive for autonomy as misbehavior they try to curb it, sometimes resorting to harsh discipline or becoming entangled in a power struggle with the child (never a good thing at any age). If parents push really hard, they can stop the "no's" and they can win the toileting battle, but they risk leaving the child with a sense of *shame* and *doubt*. Failing to develop a sense of autonomy, the child is then ill-prepared for the next developmental stage (early elementary school) where she either takes initiative, or her insecurities increase.

Regardless of how we handle it, this time is a difficult one for parents and for children. It is one of those grief processes that parents go through. Prior to age two, parents have marveled at the wonderful new abilities that seem to develop almost overnight. And suddenly our dependent, obedient, and brilliant youngster turns on us. Who is this little monster and where is my once lovable cherub? Letting go is never easy, and this can be a difficult transition for parents and for children. There are lots of good reasons to call this period "terrible twos."

Adolescence is another difficult transition and it is especially difficult at the beginning. Middle school children (roughly ages eleven through fourteen) are just entering Erikson's stage five (ages thirteen through nineteen). During this developmental stage, a person begins to establish his or her adult identity. Erikson noted that the conflicting forces at this stage are *identity* (defining who we are) versus *identity diffusion* (failure to develop a clear sense of identity).

During these years, students struggle constantly to define who they are, what group or groups they fit into, and what career path they will follow. It is also during this time that they develop the ability to think abstractly and to develop their own moral compass. In the process, they practice mate selection (Americans call it dating) and they experiment with their physical appearance until they decide "this is who I am." In short, they use the teen years to decide on the adult that they will be.

The transition from childhood to adulthood is not an easy one. To define ourselves as an adult, we have to separate from our parents. We did this once before. Stage five finishes the drive for independence that we started during the "terrible twos." And the separation can be as difficult, or even more so, than it was back then. For some teens, defining who they are means rejecting some or all of what their parents value the most. Parents wanted a doctor; the teen aspires to be a teacher. Parents wanted a teacher; the teen chooses the Marines. Parents wanted Ralph Lauren; the teen chooses Urban Outfitters. And so on and so on.

And that is just the beginning. They still have to experiment with hairstyles, clothing, drugs, sex, and music. And they must argue about curfews, friends, activities that they are and are not allowed to do, and places they are not allowed to go. And if all this isn't enough, most teens look at parents and teachers as some sort of obsolete and alien species who, at best, must be tolerated until the child turns eighteen. They are convinced that we know little about their world and that we know even less about being a teenager.

And, of course, they're right. Well, they're half right. We know what it's like to be a teenager; we just don't know what it's like to be a teenager today. It would be nice if teens and adults could admit that we are both right, but that won't occur until this rite of passage is over.

STORM AND STRESS: A JOURNEY TO THE FAR SIDE OF THE MOON

On April 12, 1961, Soviet cosmonaut Yuri Gagarin became the first person to travel into space and return safely to earth. Knowing that the United States was falling behind its Russian rival, President Kennedy announced in May 1961 that the United States would, by the end of the decade, land a man on the moon and return him safely to Earth.

To achieve this goal, the National Aeronautics and Space Administration (NASA) designed a series of twenty missions named the Apollo Program. Apollo 8 had special significance. It was the first time a space vehicle would leave Earth's orbit, reach the moon, and attempt to return to earth. This was a dangerous mission. It took three days to reach the moon and when the spacecraft circled to the far side of the moon, all communication with Earth was lost, creating several agonizing minutes of silence.

To a greater or lesser extent, most teenagers take their own journey to the far side of the moon. At some point between ages twelve and twenty, parents become acutely aware that their child is drifting "out of parent orbit." For some, this journey to the far side of the moon is short and uneventful. They accept most of their parents' values; they continue going to church; they dress pretty much as their parents dress; they do well enough in school; and they continue to abide by family rules. They may experiment with drugs and alcohol and with sex, but they seem to find ways to maintain boundaries and to avoid serious problems.

For some families, however, the journey becomes nothing short of a battle-ground. These youngsters hit adolescence at full throttle and they encounter (and create) conflict at every turn. It begins with rejecting everything their parents hold dear. And to flex their newfound teenage muscle, they do every-thing their parents prohibit. This can be a dark and difficult time.

During the elementary school years, most of these children accepted their parents' values and beliefs. But increases in intellectual ability provide young teens with the capacity to consider other options and to reflect on a broad range of new topics. And while many teens adopt their parents' political, economic, and religious values, others opt to forge their own. For those who do not stray too far from their parents' values, adolescence may not become a terribly stressful time. At the other extreme are teenagers who reject their parents' values and, instead, adopt a value system that contradicts everything their parents stand for and believe in.

This clash of values can occur over important issues (like religion or the value of an education) or it can be over more frivolous things (food choices, clothing styles, hair, and makeup). The degree of difficulty depends on the issues that separate parents and children, and how parents respond to their children's sometimes irritating efforts to define themselves.

Parents are wise to accept with amusement many of their teen's less harm-ful declarations of independence ("I am a vegan") and save their energy and patience for the important stuff. In all cases, keep in mind that most declara-tions of independence are relatively harmless attempts to define themselves. Resist the temptation to turn them into anything else.

When parents and teens clash over issues of substance (e.g., religion, known or suspected substance use/abuse, academic underachievement, gender identity), adolescence can quickly descend into a time of "storm and stress." And while 80 percent of adolescents get through these years without major difficulties,[5] families who experience significant conflicts in values can experi-ence wrenching divides that damage relationships, sometimes irreparably.

In addition to more intense conflicts with parents, teens who reject their parents' fundamental values do have a more difficult time of it. They are, for example, at increased risk for engaging in high-risk behaviors (smok-ing, drugs, early sex, fast driving, and excessive electronic media use). Not surprisingly, these behaviors become additional wedge issues that further separate parents and teens and add more fuel to the fire.

Interestingly, one of our country's first child psychologists, G. Stanley Hall (1844–1924), referred to adolescence as a time of "storm and stress." In some ways, Hall was correct. In 1904, he published an encyclopedic, two-volume set in which he explained the unique features of young people between the ages of fourteen and twenty-four. Though there are some cultural biases (his was a Victorian view and it was infused with the attitude of racial superiority that permeated Western Europe's worldview at the time), much of what he describes is consistent with current notions of adolescence.

For example, Hall noted that there was a prevalence of depressed mood during adolescence, that adolescents had increased rates of high sensation-seeking behavior, and that a high percentage of crimes were committed by adolescents. Adolescents were also more susceptible to media influences (it was newspapers and cheap novels back then) and to the influence of peers. Though he was accurate about many aspects pertaining to adolescents (the term teenager would not appear for another forty years), his ideas reflected his Victorian worldview.

One of these Victorian notions was that as children develop they recapitulate the stages of development of our species. That is, they start as untamed savages (his word) and they gradually become more civilized through training and discipline.

Hall also acknowledged that part of this taming occurred during adolescence, a time when they were more likely to be resistant or downright oppositional toward parents and teachers. Hence, he described this time as one of "storm and stress," partly to describe what was happening to the child and partly to describe the parenting difficulties associated with training a group that was not going to comply without a struggle.

AN INCREASINGLY DIFFERENTIATED (I.E., INDEPENDENT) SELF

In the century since the publication of Hall's book, however, research in human development and the neurosciences have combined to alter the way we view adolescence. The most radical change is that we now see the adolescent years as a distinct period of human development. That adolescence coincides with puberty is not surprising inasmuch as the hormonal changes associated with puberty are what sculpt the adolescent brain.

And it is this "new brain" that expresses the attitudes and behaviors associated with this stage of development, attitudes and behaviors that often conflict with parental values and parental expectations. But it is also the brain that will lead, eventually, to an adult brain by the time we reach our mid-twenties.

We have also learned that the adolescent journey to the far side of the moon may not be as bad or as difficult as we once thought. Granted, for some teens (maybe 20–30 percent) this journey is a descent into Hades where real and permanent dangers await them. But for the overwhelming majority, adolescence is more like one of those monster roller coaster rides, sometimes scary, sometimes fun, scary to watch, scarier to do. And, after all the fun and all the fright, we return to where we started.

Rather than a descent into Hades, the roller coaster ride is, we believe, a more fitting metaphor for all the confusion, disagreements, arguing, and heartbreaks of our children's teen years. But, as Mike Bradley reminds us, adolescence is like the other stages we have been through with our children. Remember when you thought middle of the night feedings and diapers was the worst thing you had ever experienced and you were convinced it would never end? So it is with adolescence.

Rather than "storm and stress," most now view adolescence as a period of healthy exploration during which teens try on all manner of "possible selves." If you saw the Harry Potter movies, you recall that the sorting hat had the ability to determine where each student fit best. Think of adolescence as a ten-year sorting hat.

Robert Marcia, a well-known child psychologist, writes that this period of intense exploration leads eventually to personal commitments. The good news in all of this is that most teens (and parents) survive adolescence without significant or long-term damage. But even for those who seem to sail through without major setbacks, the transition from childhood to adulthood is not without its challenges.

To begin with, there are the mood changes, when the happiness of childhood gives way to the depression of adolescence. Second, many teens are embarrassed by the sudden, expected, and—in many cases—unwanted body changes (squeaky voices, body and facial hair, weight gain, pimples). Third, they are exposed to all manner of temptation (drugs, alcohol, sex) associated with this "rite of passage." And, of course, there is the unrelenting peer pressure to conform.

Another problem that makes life worse for teens has to do with their mood. Negative emotions gradually increase from early to middle adolescence. Along with all the physical changes that are occurring, a more negative view makes teenagers more self-conscious, more awkward, and more easily embarrassed. They really are feeling more anxious, lonelier, and more ignored. Such changes affect all teens, but teens who suffer more significant discord with their parents tend to experience more frequent and more intense mood disturbance.

Teens are stimulation seekers. One of their most frequent mantras is "I am sooooo bored." And they really are. Well, not really bored. That's just what they call it. What they mean is that they are under-stimulated and they can't stand it when they are not being stimulated. The reason is simple. During adolescence, our brains seem to be a little short of dopamine, the primary neurotransmitter of the brain's reward system. Thrill seeking and novelty seeking cause the brain to produce more dopamine and this feels good.

And last, but certainly not least, today's teens have all those electronic gadgets. The average teenager spends approximately five hours per day engaged in various forms of electronic media (cell phones, video games, television, and social networking sites). Though some of the time spent in this electronic buffet is beneficial (such as Internet use for homework assignments), most of the time our children devote to these activities is either ill spent or wasted. It is ill spent if teens are indulging in the thousands of pornography sites currently available or they are engaging in relational aggression or if they are engaging in cyber-bullying.

As important as it is to make sure that teens are not engaging in prohibited or questionable activities, it is just as important to recognize that all of these electronic activities may add up to a monumental waste of time. As miraculous as these technologies are, they are still used mainly for recreational and entertainment purposes.

A recent study conducted by the Nielsen organization found that there has been a 43 percent increase in Facebook and Twitter use, a 12 percent increase in online video games, and a 10 percent increase in online movie viewing. All other electronic activities (e.g., e-mail, instant messaging, auctions) showed declines in use during the same time period.[6] Every hour that is spent texting, talking, viewing (videos), and playing (video games) is one hour less studying, practicing, exercising, being with other family members, and assisting with the duties of managing a home. And while studying, practicing, and exercising lead to increased competence, time spent on electronics improves nothing (except playing, viewing, and texting).

It is important to remember that during adolescence, there is a process of pruning wherein the brain eliminates synaptic connections it is not using and preserves those that are used. If, therefore, teenagers are spending the majority of their time at the electronic buffet, their brains will prune back the connections they are not using (athletic abilities, musicianship, artistic abilities, academic development) and build circuits used for electronic gadgets.

There is nothing inherently wrong with electric devices or with electronic media. As with all other tools, it is how they are used that matters. A number of political careers lay in ruin due to misuse of a cell phone. But cell phones are also used to save lives. Likewise, social networking sites like Facebook are an ideal medium for cyber-bullying, but the same technology gives parents another way to stay in touch with their children.

The transition from childhood to adulthood that we call adolescence poses special challenges for teens and parents alike. It's certainly not new. Socrates was said to complain about the youth of ancient Athens when he stated:

> The children now love luxury; they have bad manners, contempt for authority; they show disrespect for elders and love chatter in place of exercise. Children are now tyrants, not the servants of their households. They no longer rise when elders enter the room. They contradict their parents, chatter before company, gobble up dainties at the table, cross their legs, and tyrannize their teachers.[7]

Even cultures we generally think of as conservative acknowledge this special period of development. In Amish communities, for example, there is the tradition known as *rumspringa*.[8] Loosely translated, *rumspringa* means "running around." It begins when a teenager reaches his or her sixteenth birthday and ends in marriage sometime between ages nineteen and twenty-one.

Rumspringa provides Amish adolescents the opportunity to explore the world outside their church community without the close supervision of parents. In a way, this is the Amish version of the trip to the far side of the moon. In addition to exploration, *rumspringa* also is a time of identity formation. After *rumspringa*, should the person choose to leave the Amish community, they are free to do so. No one is forced to join the church community, not even those born into it. Thus, they use this time to determine their adult identity.

Across time and across cultures, adolescence represents a challenging transition for children and parents. A changing brain complicates immeasurably the already difficult task of identity formation. In a rather ironic twist, brain changes started at puberty impel individuals to leave home, to take risks, to seek new adventures. At the same time, however, the part of the brain that contains these urges is not yet ready to inhibit and to moderate these urges.

Eventually, the hormones will come into balance, the synaptic connections will become more efficient, and the brain's inhibitory mechanisms will develop and mature. In the interim, adolescents struggle—with themselves, their parents, and their teachers—to figure out who they are and who they are going to be. In the chapters that follow, we will get a taste of what this struggle looks like.

Chapter 5

Unusual Choices They Make

Middle school youngsters often make unusual choices throughout their early teen years. While some of these choices are understandable, others are simply incomprehensible to adults. What causes our middle school youth to do the things they do? Why do they react the way they do? In the chapters that follow, real-life stories from various middle schools will be shared and discussed. The names and sometimes the genders, and some specific details have been changed as a way of protecting the identity of students and families.

HE ATE THE FROG HEART!

One early afternoon it was brought to the principal's attention that one of her students had eaten a frog heart at lunch. Earlier in the day students in Life Science had dissected frogs and on a dare from another student, Peter had decided that he would bring the frog's heart to lunch and eat it to prove that "he was a man."

Mrs. Callahan, the principal, asked two girls who had witnessed the event to come to the office and write their testimonies about what they had just seen. The girls were still writing as Peter triumphantly marched down the office hallway toward Mrs. Callahan. She looked at him as seriously as she could and asked, "Well, did you do it? Did you eat the frog heart?"

Peter replied, "Yes, ma'am, I did."

She responded, "Why would you eat a frog heart?"

"I got twenty dollars for it as a dare. That's why," he grinned.

She couldn't understand it. She told him that they would have to call Poison Control and his parents and that he might be throwing up in the near future. His response: "It was all worth it!"

During their conversation, the guidance counselor was in an adjacent conference room where Mrs. Callahan could see her, but Peter couldn't. As the counselor listened to the story, she looked at Mrs. Callahan and began to quietly laugh. Her laughter did not help the situation as the principal knew she had to hold it together, even though a frog heart was in a student's stomach.

Mrs. Callahan continued to talk to Peter and then asked him, "Who gave you the twenty dollars?" He admitted that Sally had made the lucrative offer.

"Well," she responded, "we need to get Sally down here right away."

At this point, the guidance counselor burst into laughter. Tears were streaming down her cheeks, as she pointed at one of the girls writing in the same room and said, "That would be your girl right over there." The principal's shock and the sight of her guidance counselor losing it and laughing during a discipline case seemed too much to handle.

Mrs. Callahan looked at Sally and said, "And you're writing against him right now on your paper? Why didn't you tell me this?" Finally the girl explained, "Well, I didn't know how to tell you so I was going to write it to you."

So, now the principal had one student who had ingested a frog heart, the student who dared him and offered him money and was now testifying against him, and a guidance counselor unable to control her laughter. At this point, even Mrs. Callahan was beginning to see the humor in this, but she had to maintain that "don't laugh now" look.

When the principal called the parents, one mom laughed and one did not. There were two different responses from two different parents, although both were friendly and amiable as to how it was handled.

HIS HAIR IS ON FIRE!

A high school assistant principal was asked to teach a summer remedial English middle school class. She had never had any experience with middle schoolers but welcomed the opportunity to grow and to learn about this age group. Little did she know that this particular group of eighth grade remedial students had already caused several other teachers to "go by the wayside" after they had experienced this particular summer school course with this rambunctious group of students. They were a challenge, to say the least.

After instructing for a little while, she turned to write on the board. When she turned back around, she discovered one of the youngsters, coincidentally with bright red hair, sitting there with his hair on fire! He had the very fashionable afro hairdo and it was literally aflame! She ran to his aid, tearing her sweater off to use it to beat out the flames on his head. After the fire was extinguished, she questioned the young man behind him who sat there with a cigarette lighter. "Why would you do that?" she asked.

He looked up at her, staring blankly into her face, and responded very solemnly "I couldn't see." She of course delivered him to the principal's office, threatening the rest of the middle schoolers not to get out of their seats, but to remain seated and continue to work. After all, this was a middle school student who decided he needed to handle the situation himself, as they often want to do, without much common sense attached to the decision.

HIS HAND WAS STUCK IN THE CHAIR!

Mrs. Smith, the guidance counselor, was doubled over with laughter as she talked about what had happened with one of their tall and husky seventh graders. While in math class, he had wondered if his hand would fit through the middle of the three openings in the back of his chair. He managed to maneuver his hand into the opening but found he could not withdraw it.

When Mrs. Smith arrived at the classroom, it was evident that the teacher had lost a bit of the classroom control. Students were laughing and blurting out loud about the comical scene that had just developed in the back of the room. The young man continued to struggle to free his hand that was being held captive in his chair while the teacher growing more upset with him. The students watched the event unfold with wide eyes, laughing when they felt they could get away with it.

The math teacher was quite distressed, chanting to the students, "This is not funny!" over and over. The guidance counselor began to whisper, "Yes, it is funny . . ." and proceeded to walk him down the second-floor hallway with a large green chair attached to the student's hand overhead, ducking as they came to doorways.

She knew they could get it off, but not without some kind of lubricant. Why had he decided to do this? When the principal arrived at the clinic, there he was getting his hand greased with Vaseline. The student was smiling, proud of his unusual accomplishment. He didn't mind the attention at all. The assistant principal took his picture on his cell phone for posterity. Why not? They wanted to remember these times . . . times spent with middle school youth who seem to revel in awkward happenings that bring them fame.

I NEED TO BE ADOPTED TODAY—FREE SHIPPING

There he was, standing by the car rider line in the morning as the parents were dropping off their students. He didn't mind showing how he felt for the day. Why would he? He was a middle school student. On a cardboard sign he had written "I need to be adopted today. Free shipping." On the other side of the homemade sign he had added, "Will work for food." He was currently living with his grandparents and honestly wanted to go back and live with his parents. However, it wasn't possible at the time. Using humor, he delivered his message and also impressed his peers with his jovial attitude while looking for a new home.

When the principal talked to him about it later, of course he thought he was in trouble. However, he wasn't in trouble. He only really needed to talk about how he felt about his current situation. When asked if he had any takers before he was told to stop, he responded, "Yes, but then she drove off." For him, making others laugh while sharing his feelings made him feel accomplished and good about himself and gave him the means to deal with difficult parental circumstances. He is not alone in facing such situations.

BATHROOM DECORATIONS

It happens every once in a while. A student reports to the office to share the news that a bathroom has been decorated with toilet paper. It is hanging from the stalls, soaked in the sinks and then placed strategically on the walls and the toilet seats. What students don't remember are the security cameras which clearly show the students who were going in and out of the bathroom at the time of the "crime."

One day an eighth grade student decided to write inappropriate comments about a specific teacher in the sixth grade wing. Only one eighth grade foreign language class was held in the building and the note on the bathroom wall was about this one eighth grade Spanish teacher. Apparently, Johnny didn't think that anyone would figure that out. Middle schoolers often think they can get away with all sorts of behavior, not realizing they leave so many clues for the administrators tasked with solving the "crime."

Johnny was one of only ten eighth grade boys who entered that wing for this one Spanish class. Already the details of who had creatively written about the teacher were narrowed down to ten boys due to the location of the bathroom and the wing it was in. After investigating and studying the handwriting, the mystery was solved and a consequence was given. Why do they make these choices at this age and why do they think they will not get caught?

THIRSTY

It was time for the bell to ring at the end of the day. The students were packing up their belongings when the rain began to descend like a blanket of water on the school campus. Principal Jones was headed out the door to ensure the safety of all of his students during dismissal time. Every administrator hopes the rain will stay away during dismissal time. However, today was going to be one of those days when the middle schoolers were a bit more challenging to deal with because of the inclement weather.

As Mr. Jones headed for the bus area zone he passed through the outdoor hallways where aluminum roofs covered the sidewalks. Water was gushing out of the rain spouts that were strategically placed along the covered walkways. As Mr. Jones quickly walked to the bus area, he noticed Joey, a seventh grade student, lying flat on his back on the sidewalk under the covered pathway. Joey's face was looking right up into the end of one of the rain spouts and water was pouring all over his head.

Mr. Jones abruptly stopped to ask Joey what in the world he was doing! The young man looked up at the principal and with a big grin on his face responded, "I was thirsty." The surprised but not shocked Mr. Jones proceeded down the walkway to the bus area. He knew that this was the world he lived in, a world of middle-level students who made decisions that at times were difficult to understand.

PAPER EATER

No one knew why he did it and the art teacher wasn't able to stop him. Salvatore would eat any paper he could get his hands on in art. It might be tissue paper, construction paper, or regular drawing paper. Ms. Samples would ask him not to eat the art paper, but Salvatore just felt the need to chew away whenever he could get away with it.

Salvatore even turned in his work with corners missing that he had torn off to enjoy as a feast. Yummy! He could hardly resist the scrumptious taste of the different types of art paper. Why would a middle school student feel the need to chew paper while working on his art projects?

WHY THEY DO WHAT THEY DO

These stories are the classic tales of middle school students. Though the circumstances differ from story to story, there are some common early adolescent themes running through all of them. First, all of these youngsters felt an urge to do something. It's often said that middle school students are not motivated. Oh, they are motivated all right. They may not be motivated to do what parents and teachers ask, but they are motivated. What motivation, you ask? Remember puberty? Well that flood of hormones is not just about reproductive capacity. Those hormones also motivate us to action.

If nothing else, teens are motivated to get their needs met. And they want to get their needs met immediately. Why wait? I want it and I want it now. Thirsty? Lie down and take a swig from the lawn sprinklers. Can't see around the kid's hair in front of you? Set it on fire and get it out of the way. The water's not potable? The fire might injure my classmate? The ability to anticipate consequences is the responsibility of our frontal lobes; at age twelve or thirteen, your frontal lobes are not up to the task.

What of the boy seeking adoption? Lots of teenage stuff going on here. First, this is the time when teens emigrate, when they begin moving away from family and toward peers. He was taking the first step, moving away from family. Granted, his home situation was not typical. But even when we live with our parents, there comes a time when we feel the urge to leave. It is an essential part of establishing our own identity. That he added a humorous twist is also typical.

Freud often said that there are no jokes. Humor provides a more socially acceptable way of expressing some of our deepest feelings. Make a joke of your circumstances, even when those very circumstances are crushing you. What this boy really wanted was to talk to someone about his circumstances. He knew the sign wouldn't get him adopted. But maybe, just maybe, someone might take the time to let him talk about his circumstances.

As for the paper eater, there are several possibilities. As most teachers know, students who eat nonfood items may be suffering from a condition called pica. Pica is not all that unusual in children between one and six years of age, when as many as 30 percent of children will consume nonfood items.[9] In older children, however, pica can be associated with nutritional deficiencies and some types of psychopathology.

Recent TV programs have provided graphic descriptions of people who eat chalk, cleanser, laundry detergent, and other nonfood items. Less serious but still of concern is the fact that some students chew on items because it relieves stress and anxiety. Before attributing this student's behavior to attention getting, it is prudent to first make sure that it is not symptomatic of another, more serious disorder. Remember, it is our job to keep them safe.

What about the boy who ate the frog heart? What was he thinking? Well, he wasn't thinking, at least not in the way adults use the term. Rather, he was following his urges. What urges? The urge to take a risk (and stimulate dopamine production), the urge to impress his classmates and to demonstrate what he is made of (identity formation). And the urge to make a little spending money (because when a teenager senses the possibility of a reward, the possibility of something bad happening does not get factored into the equation).

What about the fact that the frog heart is preserved with formaldehyde and other cancer-causing chemicals? Oops!! There go my frontal lobes again!

And the bathroom decorator? Okay, let's be fair. Would it occur to most middle schoolers that you are the only eighth grade group in this sixth grade wing? Not likely. But if you were about to commit an offense, you would assume that the student would consider the consequences. However, this kind of insightful thinking is in short supply if you have excess GABA receptors and too much white matter.

Okay, maybe that level of reasoning requires too much thinking, but what about the security cameras? You know there are cameras in the hallways, right? What were you thinking? Well maybe, just a little. Fortunately, it is temporary. Once my white matter gets pruned back and some of the GABA receptors die off (by about age fifteen or sixteen), I'll be more intelligent.

Why do young teens make decisions that seem so illogical to adults? Mainly it's because of the way their brains are working, or, more precisely, how they are not working. As noted earlier, the emotional parts of the brain are working just fine and students tend to act on these emotions. Unfortunately, the brain's inhibitory mechanisms are unable to keep up with their actions. Rather than thinking about consequences, adolescents focus solely on getting what they need or want.

Chapter 6

Predicaments They Get Themselves Into

A DROP TO THE KNEES

Mrs. Sampson, the principal, remembers a young man who was always getting into trouble. She never knew what to expect. He wasn't a mean student at all, actually very likable; he just didn't make wise decisions. He was born in another country and had cultural differences that made him react to situations differently. Not all of his family members spoke English, so at times the school personnel had a tough time communicating their concerns and thoughts.

José had gotten into trouble again and Mrs. Sampson was having a heart-to-heart conversation with him, even though she was doing most of the talking. She shared that she really didn't know why he thought it was all right to do what he had done. The student continued to stare at the principal, not saying much, as she went on with what she thought should be his next course of action in doing the right thing at school.

All of a sudden, without any notice, he dropped to his knees and covered his face. Mrs. Sampson stopped and stared. There he was, head down, hands tightly clasped together and not making a sound. She asked him, "What are you doing? We're talking here." Silence continued. She asked again, "José, what are you doing? I need to talk to you."

Suddenly, José lifted his head up and looked at her very seriously. Eye to eye, he sternly responded with complete indignation, "Hey, I'm praying. Do you have a problem with that?"

Mrs. Sampson couldn't believe it. She had not experienced a student dropping to his knees to pray while she was talking to him, especially a student who often chose to get into mischief.

She had to leave the room. She couldn't hold in the laughter. Mrs. Sampson held it together and without responding to his question, walked directly to the guidance counselor's office, closed the door, and began to laugh as quietly as possible. One of the secretaries was on the other side of the glass partition and had heard it all. The secretary lowered her head to collapse into silent laughter. Middle school students are quite entertaining! The young man needed to pray and he needed to do it right away, even if his principal was talking to him at the moment.

HOLD THE CAN

As Mrs. Everett, the principal, watched him vomit in the garbage can, she wondered how this office referral could have affected him in this way. She had just called down one of their seventh graders to talk to him about a phone call she had received. Another student's parent had called to say that Joe had threatened to push her child over the cliff at the field trip. (Note: there were no cliffs in this area.)

Joe's feelings had been hurt on the field trip by this young man: he had not picked Joe as his field trip partner, and Joe was devastated by the rejection. As a result, Joe quickly decided to threaten his friend with a push off of a cliff. Joe had even been grinning when he had threatened his buddy, but at that moment he felt like justice had been served and he was getting even with his close friend.

When Mrs. Everett called Joe down, he began to sob uncontrollably, saying he didn't mean it and that he would never throw his close good friend off a cliff. She finally calmed him down and asked him to write what had happened while she went out to find the two other students who had witnessed the event. Mrs. Everett returned down the hall to hear the secretary saying Joe really needed her.

She returned to find Joe crying, tears rolling down his face, saying he was going to throw up. Joe was thin-framed, wore glasses and was really a good student who had just made a mistake with what he had said. As Mrs. Everett held out the trash can, she thought, "This is my life, holding out a can for upset students. I really do love my job, right? Right!"

STUDENTS WRITE

Principals at times receive letters or e-mails from students who want to share how they are feeling at the moment with the administration. Some may write an apology note, some start a petition and ask to come and meet with the principal over an issue they see as serious, and some write a note about a concern they have. Here are a few samples, with the students' spelling and grammar preserved:

Dear Principal,

I am very regretful of what I have done. I learned a good lesson. I had to go and work in the orange groves on Wednesday and on Thursday. I had to cut all of the weeds out of our lake and then go back to the orange groves. I think that I have learned to stay away from people doing stupid stuff. I promise that it won't ever happen again. I did not mean for someone to get hurt, I just took it as a joke. From now on I will stay away from all the stupid ideas that my friends have. It will never happen again.

Dear Principal,

What I should have done when you asked me to come to the office was actually go and talk to you. I know what I did was wrong and I am sorry for not obeying your orders. I guess I just wanted to look cool in front of my friends but I know now that next time you tell me to do something I will do it. I don't care what my friends think. For that I am sorry and I will never disobey your orders again.

(Turned in to our "Bully Box" in the office): Robbie Jones repeatedly bent the truth on a matter that I missaid completely. I said he could be the next Internet Celebrity. He took it the wrong way and said he would take it up with the principal. I said I would have my dad here to defend my case. He took that the wrong way and he said he would have charges filed against me for verbal abuse. He has done this too many times. This concludes this description.

STUDENT EMAILS TO PRINCIPAL

Students would sometimes write Mrs. Smith, the principal, with suggestions, questions, and concerns. They might wonder what the appropriate dress was for an upcoming dance or they might propose an idea of starting a new club. One young man decided to wait until mid- summer to share his concerns with the principal. He began by asking the principal if there was any way he could have gotten the wrong grades on his report card. Mrs. Smith assured him that his grades were probably correct as the teachers verify the grades before report cards are sent out.

He persisted, saying that he had some pretty bad grades on his report card. The principal asked if he had been promoted to the next grade level and he responded that he had. After discovering that he had passed, she once again told him that indeed those grades were his. He promptly ended the mail by saying okay and thanked her for her time.

STANDING OUTSIDE DURING DUTY TIME

Mrs. Patten, the assistant principal, was outside in the morning, waiting for the students to enter their first period classrooms. They still had a few students in the hallways and in the outside courtyard area. Standing outside at the top of the stairs, Mrs. Patten began to hear two young female students repeat the same word over and over as they walked toward their classroom in the middle of the picnic table area. "Sex, sex, sex, sex . . ." over and over was what the girls were saying.

She called out to them, "Stop, girls! Why are you saying that?"

They responded, "Our school nurse kept saying it during our nurse education lessons the other day. It disturbed us!"

Mrs. Patten responded, "Well, you're disturbing me now!" They giggled and went on to class.

HERE'S MY REPORT CARD

The parents had come to discuss with Mr. Simpson, the assistant principal, their concerns about their son's lack of success at the school. Jeff was just not getting the grades he needed. As they discussed what could be done about it, Mr. Simpson looked at the young man and asked him if he had given his report card to his parents. Jeff shared that he was getting ready to do this, but hadn't had the opportunity to give his report card to them yet. Mr. Simpson asked him where it was, and Jeff responded that he had been saving it for his parents and would be giving it to them soon.

Still no report card in sight, the administrator inquired as to the whereabouts of this very important document and if Jeff knew when he would be giving it to them. He responded that he had it in his pocket ready to go. At this point Mr. Simpson asked him if he would hand it over to his astonished mom and dad. Jeff promptly reached into his pocket and pulled out a tiny, tightly bound and hardened balled-up piece of blue paper that was around one inch in diameter.

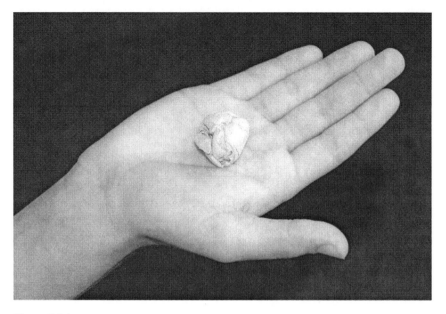

Figure 6.1.

Apparently the report card had gone through the washing machine and the dryer and could not be opened, because of the new composition it had taken. Even though the balled-up report card was not readable, the student felt he had it ready to go for his parents and was waiting for just the right moment to share it.

WHY THEY DO WHAT THEY DO

These are the typical predicaments that middle school students seem to find so effortlessly. There are a couple of general comments worth making before discussing the individual episodes. First, no serious harm was done by any of these missteps. No one was injured, no property was destroyed, and learning was not interrupted.

Second, most of these students expressed sincere remorse for their actions. These are typical teens. Most are not dangerous or destructive and they really do care about what their parents, teachers, and principals think of them. Yes, they are sometimes a little silly and they don't always think of the consequences, but they do not intentionally hurt anyone and they really are sorry when they are disobedient or when they break rules.

The strangest case here is the boy who dropped to his knees to pray while his principal was trying to talk to him. Why did he do this? Who knows? To escape the principal's wrath? To avoid a lecture? To avoid a confession? One might say the spirit moved him, and that would be correct. Once the idea struck him that it would be an appropriate time to pray, he simply dropped to his knees. And what do we know about such actions in young teens? That once the thought occurs to them, chances are it will turn into action, because the frontal lobes aren't very good at inhibiting such impulsive behaviors.

That story about Joe threatening to throw his friend off a cliff is also a classic. As the principal notes, there are no cliffs in this area. And Joe didn't really have any intention of throwing his friend anywhere. It is hyperbole — something teens engage in regularly. Hyperbole + no impulse control = outlandish threats.

Joe did the best he could with the verbal skills he possesses. And with hurt feelings, he was resorting to hot cognitions to decide what to do about this situation. His feelings were hurt and he wanted his friend to know it. A few years from now, he will be better able to explain his reaction to his friend using cool cognitions and complete sentences. But those language, cognitive, and self-control skills are a few years off.

The letters and e-mails to the principal provide a window into an important aspect of adolescent thinking. In each case, these are sincere apologies. Sure, the writing style is a little rough, with numerous spelling and usage errors, but it is, as some might say, the thought that counts. And the thought here is sincere and heartfelt. They really care what the principal thinks about them. And they care about what their parents think. Parents and teachers wrongly assume that they no longer matter to the youngsters in their charge. But they do care. As the letters in chapter 13 show, they care deeply; they don't admit it publicly, but they care.

Sex, sex, sex. Is that all they think about? Of course it isn't. They have too many other concerns to worry about. Then what were these girls thinking? Oops, that's right; they weren't. They were expressing. Teens find it easy to express themselves, especially when there are peers around to provide moral support. That these girls were yelling "sex" in the school yard is not surprising. They have to get the energy out somehow, and yelling sex repeatedly works just fine, thank you.

One other thing to notice: With just a minimum of redirecting, the girls stopped. No challenges, no opposition. They did as they were asked, emphasis on asked. Had they been challenged and threatened, who knows how they would have interpreted the principal's facial expression. And if they interpreted her face incorrectly, they might have challenged the principal, and then there would be problems. As it is, the principal simply reminded the girls that the boundaries were still there.

And finally, the report card. Did he have something to hide? Maybe, but does it matter? There was a time when the only report card was the one that was sent home for parent signature. Students had to have it signed and returned, as that was the only copy. With copying machines and computers, however, there are copies all over. So it is no big deal that Jeff lost his report card.

But there are essential features of adolescence that come percolating to the top of this situation. First, one has to wonder if Jeff really thought that by getting his report card destroyed, he might be able to escape whatever consequences he believed were waiting for him. Never mind that he only bought himself one or two days. Teens live in the here and now. A few days is a long time and maybe some miracle will happen and change everything. A little fantasy, but that's how they think.

And second, this story reminds us that sometimes, through no fault of their own, bad things happen to assignments. Work gets left on kitchen counters where it virtually ensures that there will be a coffee spill. Or it is left on the floor where the family dog can use it as a chew toy. Yes, it is true: sometimes the dog really does eat homework. This is not to offer students an excuse; rather it is a way to tell students you understand that they are human and that you are willing to trust them. Better to be taken advantage of once in a while than to damage a relationship over one homework assignment.

By nature early teenagers are not good problem solvers. They will eventually get there, but in the process they are going to make numerous mistakes. One of their biggest problems is that they live in the present and they typically opt for short-term gain. They are also ruled by emotions, and if they sense the possibility of a reward they virtually disregard the possibility of negative consequences.

Chapter 7

As a Group They Want to Be Heard

BINDERS NEED STRAPS!

According to the school's policy, binders were required at the school, but they were not to have long shoulder straps that looked more like backpacks. It had been decided that this was a safety issue. Backpacks were to be left in the lockers during the day and only binders with no straps would be carried around the school.

A ten-page student petition began circulating around the school, generated by an articulate sixth grader with a thin frame, glasses, and a soft but clear voice. She appeared at the principal's office, petition in hand, to persuade whoever she needed to convince that binders needed shoulder straps. Besides having quite a long list of student concerns about the required binders, drawings were included that showed the spinal cord being damaged due to the use of a zippered binder that had no shoulder strap. The petition was titled "Why Not to Get Rid of Binders with Handles—The Argument and Voice of the Students."

The first graphic included a drawing of the backbone on the first day of school. Various parts of the body were labeled to explain the drawing: student, backbone, waist, and binder. The next page showed a backbone that was twisted due to the student in the drawing having to carry a binder all year with no shoulder strap. The word *problem* was at the end of an arrow that pointed to the bent backbone.

Students had not only signed the document, but they added comments that told of their disdain for the strapless binders. John told of his struggle with

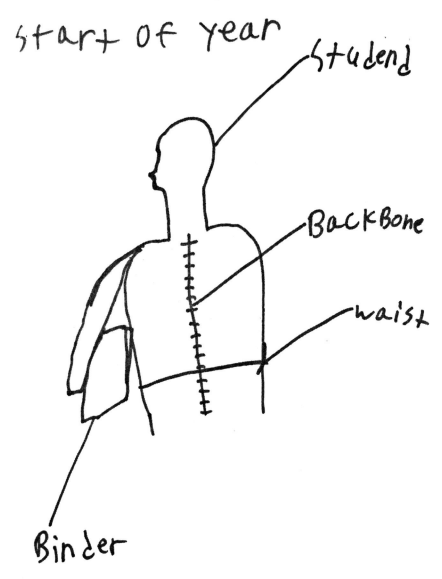

Figure 7.1.

keeping his supplies together, because his binder would burst apart. Ricky wanted straps to assist with lowering his parents' chiropractic bills. Jimmy felt that the binders with straps would be far more convenient for the students. Sally insisted that a binder with straps wasn't a backpack and that it truly was just a binder. Sam told of breaking his binder because he had to overstuff it.

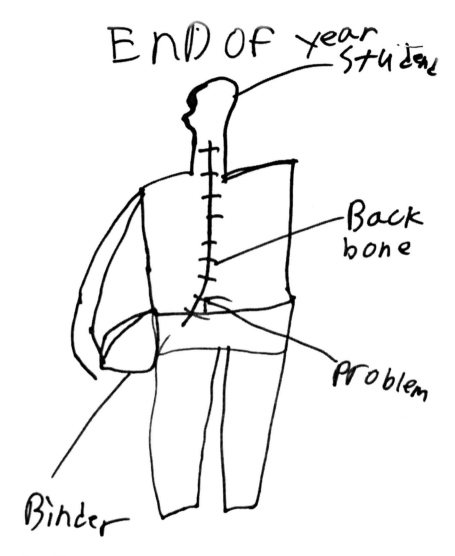

Figure 7.2.

Finally, Allison felt sure that these binders with straps would be the absolute future!

Although the policy was not changed, the sixth grader certainly gave it her best shot. At the end of the day, the students still had to put their backpacks and larger bags that had the long straps in their lockers during the day. However, she felt better as she had been heard and had presented her reasons as to why she wanted it changed. Middle school students want to be heard and they are even willing to collect signatures if needed.

THE LUNCHROOM

The rumor was out on one particular day that the seventh graders had not behaved very well in the cafeteria during lunchtime. So often when this happens, they encourage each other to display inappropriate behavior they wouldn't normally do individually. For instance, after the adult in charge speaks, a few students might begin to laugh or applaud for some reason and they then influence others in the group to also contribute to the unruly behavior. It had happened while the principal was not in the lunchroom and something had to be done.

Upon hearing the news, Mrs. Smith made an announcement over the intercom system that all seventh graders must return to the lunchroom. They would discuss what had just happened after lunch and would then hear what would occur from this point forward. The students filed into the cafeteria, all amazed and a bit surprised that they were called out of class to hear the principal's speech. One could sense the seriousness in the air. The teachers, who normally might try to take the few minutes to catch up on something and not come in to listen, were also all in attendance to hear the admonition.

Students were asked to take a seat and to look directly at the principal. No one spoke a word. Gradually, as Mrs. Smith shared her disappointment with their behavior and relayed her expectations of how seventh grade lunchtime should be, a slow-moving body of water began to move across the floor of the cafeteria. The water slowly but steadily began to cover the floor. No one expected this nor understood what was happening, but the principal valiantly continued her speech. Gradually middle school feet began to pop up, suspended in the air, to prevent their shoes from getting soaked as the water moved along the floor halfway across the lunchroom.

Although Mrs. Smith noticed the water and tried to remain stern with her students, she was also wondering why there was water on the floor. It was hard to stay composed due to the unusual nature of what was occurring, but she needed to press on. At the end of the session, the students were asked to be careful as they left the cafeteria, using caution due to the water, never previously mentioned, that covered the floor. Apparently the new bathroom that had just been added to the cafeteria was built on the sprinkler system. A county maintenance worker had come to school to check out the system and turned it on during this important event.

Even though as a group the students had made the decision to act inappropriately, as a group they had also made the appropriate choice to listen and behave even when faced with the unusual situation of being present while the room flooded.

THEY MOURN AS A GROUP

Cindy was a vivacious and popular seventh grader that everyone seemed to know and love. She was funny, caring, and encouraging, a real leader. One day after school she was involved in a motor vehicle accident that took her life. Her school family began to mourn.

Crisis teams reported to the school the next morning. The students created signs that they used to decorate her locker. Students displayed pictures of her on her locker with notes sharing how much they cared for her. Small groups of young people gathered in different areas of the school to meet in groups to mourn the loss of their dear friend and to work with volunteer counselors. Poems were written by students and shared on the intercom. Students made up large cards for Cindy's family and a special area in the garden was designated where the school family planted a tree just for Cindy.

As a group, they mourned. They shared how they felt and cried for hours during school time. Education stopped until they healed. As a group, they supported each other and let others hear and see how much they hurt. They felt a great loss and supported each other through the tough time by being there for each other.

PETITION TO FIRE THE TEACHER

It happens every once in a while in the school setting that a group of students decide it is in their best interest to draw up a petition to have a specific teacher fired. Parents have not complained, but for some reason, the students feel it is the thing to do. During this one incident, the rumor was going around that the petition was going from one student to another. Mr. Jones just had to go! He was older and just didn't seem to connect with the students.

The assistant principal collected the pages of signatures and suggested that the students stop the petition. The petition read, "We the undersigned request this teacher be fired." The school doesn't usually make a big issue of the petitions. They are collected, considered, and then filed. On this occasion, the teacher never found out that the petition went around the school. He was doing a good job, but for some reason had not pleased a particular group of students at that time. As a group, students can feel very empowered.

DARTS

None of the adults knew what was happening but they were seeing the eighth graders suddenly drop to the floor and sit until another student came by and touched them on the neck. Possibly hundreds of eighth graders were dropping to the floor at some point during the day. They were dropping in the cafeteria, in the classrooms, and in the hallways. Walking down the hallway, they were dropping like flies.

Students were sitting on the stairwells, waiting for the touch on the neck. It even happened in the cafeteria; Jessie fell to the floor and sat there while all of the other eighth graders proceeded past Jessie in the food line. Not even the lunchroom lady seemed concerned or noticed the planted student on the floor.

When another student froze in the art classroom, the art teacher heard him saying very quietly while not moving his lips, "Can you touch my neck?" The teacher looked quizzically at him, but couldn't understand it until other students coached her to touch his neck.

The game was called *Darts*. As a student would walk throughout the school, another student would pretend to blow a dart, while cupping his hands and blowing. This meant the other student was to drop to the floor until someone came and saved the student by touching the student's neck. Up came the student for another chance at playing the dart game.

It was finally reported to the administration, the announcement was made to stop the game, and the escapade fell apart. The staff needed everyone off of the floors and going where they needed to go. How do middle schoolers come up with such ideas and how do these spread so quickly? They are creative and social creatures who take risks to be a part of the pack. They enjoy each other's company and want to be seen as team players. They crave individuality, but they want to blend in at the same time.

SAM WAS GONE

Sam was gone. He wasn't dead, but he had been sent to another school due to his long-term misbehavior. But Sam was loved by all of the students. He was cool. He was popular. He was a leader, often not in the appropriate way but he was well accepted and admired by his peers.

When the eighth grader first came to the school, he often made the other eighth graders laugh. He was funny and was willing to take the risks that would bring him the attention he needed. When he chose to get into too many altercations, consequences were given but it did not seem to change his negative behaviors.

When the large group of eighth graders discovered that he would not be attending their school anymore, they went to work making posters of protest.

They memorialized his lunchroom seat and promised to not sit it in ever again. Teachers flocked to the principal's office to request that the signs be taken down immediately.

However, the decision was made to leave the signs in place. It demonstrated that there are consequences for inappropriate behavior. Middle schoolers take on leadership roles and their peers join forces to support their leaders. They develop their own sense of hierarchy and adults have to hope that they will make appropriate choices during this very important stage in their lives.

GIDDY UP!

The administration had asked the teachers to be sure to be standing at their doorways during hallway time. The end of the school year was drawing near and the students were excited about their impending summer vacation. Mr. Taylor's social studies classes had just finished a unit on the Oregon Trail, and he had put tape down on the floor to represent the dimensions of a Conestoga Wagon that would have been used by the early settlers. It measured four feet by twelve feet. This one particular morning, following the principal's directive, Mr. Taylor was standing at his classroom door, monitoring student behavior in the hallway between the bells.

When the bell rang, most of his social studies students were in the room. Mr. Taylor entered the room to find his students all gathered into the four by twelve foot area in the middle of the room, pretending to be the early settlers, travelling in the covered wagon. One of the students was at the front of the entourage, sitting in the teacher's rocking chair, which he had positioned very carefully at the front of the covered wagon. As a team, the students were rolling back and forth in the imaginary covered wagon while they waited for their teacher to enter the room.

They knew they should have been in their seats beginning their warm ups, but they had decided as a group to create their own "warm up" and to see if the teacher, who was complying with the principal's orders, would appreciate their efforts. He did! He laughed, found space in the wagon and joined them on their journey.

WHY THEY DO WHAT THEY DO

These stories illustrate the classic stories of adolescent affiliation and of adolescents trying to exercise some control over their lives. In chapter 6 (Predicaments They Get Themselves Into) there were several anecdotes of individuals seeking to exercise some degree of control over their lives. One student did it by praying when he should have been in conversation with his principal. A second student did so by delaying giving his parents a report card. A third emailed the principal to question the accuracy of his grades. In each case, however, they relented without much conviction or passion.

So why didn't they press their issues? Try to look at it this way: because their goal was not to win; each was simply practicing an adult role. You see, one doesn't springboard from child to adult. It is a learning process that requires practice. Just as early adolescents practice physical, musical, or artistic skills that they will use as adults, they also practice the social and language skills they will use as adults. And when do they do this practice? During adolescence, because it is during adolescence that they practice taking control of their lives.

In this chapter, we add a second dimension to control seeking: group membership. And here we have two natural tendencies converging to create what, at first, may feel like open rebellion. However, let's take a closer look. What is happening in the stories in chapter seven is completely normal behavior. In the first place, teenagers are desperately seeking to exercise some degree of control over their lives. You don't just have some arbitrary birthday and then become a self-sufficient adult. Being a self-sufficient, problem-solving, decision-making adult requires practice.

The second truth in this chapter is that adolescents affiliate with peers. In fact, on school days adolescents spend, on average, four times as much time with peers as they do with parents.[10] Increased socializing with peers is not confined to humans. Most mammals, even rodents, move outside the family unit (this is called emigration) and spend more time with peers during adolescence. That such a characteristic has been conserved suggests that emigration must have some adaptive function.

Linda Spear, Distinguished Professor at the State University of New York at Binghamtom, suggests that adolescents emigrate as a way of learning their adult roles (mainly aggression and mating) in a non-family setting. Once a member of the family reaches sexual maturity, there is something especially adaptive about moving away from the family as it protects against the genetic risks posed by inbreeding.

When you combine control taking and peer affiliation with a shared sense of justice (or injustice), you have a perfect recipe for group think, and the petitions are sure to follow. Humans are nothing if not social. From our earliest beginnings we lived in groups. And across time, isolating individuals or excluding individuals from group membership has been used as punishment.

Whether through ostracism, banishment, shunning, or being exiled, the message was clear: We no longer want you. This is a harsh rebuke that goes to the heart of one of our most basic needs, the need to associate with others.

It is why prisoners in solitary confinement often become disoriented and lose mental functions.

The urge to affiliate is life long, starting in infancy and continuing throughout a lifetime. It is not surprising that there is dramatic increase in peer socialization after puberty. Beginning in middle school and continuing through adolescence, we see youngsters beginning to replace the support, advice, and security of the family with the support, advice, and security of the group. That is, early adolescents are ready to leave the family hut, but they're not quite ready to go it alone.

This need for affiliation also explains why gang membership is so appealing to so many of our nation's young people. Lacking the support of a family, they seek it where they can get it. Quickly, the gang becomes the family. It's all about affiliation and belonging to a group.

The petitions for notebook straps, firing a teacher, and retaining a popular student reflect the added strength of group membership combined with an age-appropriate need to exercise control over one's circumstances. If we really want children to be assertive and not passive, if we want them to take charge of their lives, then we must provide them the opportunity to do so. Rather than seeing these periodic student petitions simply as resistance to adult authority, they might also be viewed as age-appropriate and normal signs of adolescents practicing to be adults.

Chapter 8

Relating to Peers and Others

HE SAID, SHE SAID

A common thread of middle school life seems to be the "he said, she said" scenario. So often, it involves several girls, but sometimes guys are involved as well. Jimmy, an innocent and younger middle schooler, had had enough of the rumors. He marched to the office to say he was done with it. Sarah had continued to spread rumors about him and Patty, a girl whom he had liked in the past. He was totally exasperated by the situation.

As he met with Mrs. Lawrence, the principal, he shared how the rumors were rampant and he needed it fixed right away. When asked if he wanted to confront the young lady, he indicated that he was more than willing to do so. Sarah was pulled from class to discuss the rumors, but when asked if she was involved, she emphatically denied any part in them. However, she shared that she believed her brother was the guilty party. As the discussion went on, Sarah admitted that she had heard the rumors, of course, and that they involved Jimmy actually meeting with Patty to determine their future, which possibly included marriage.

With much hesitation and stalling, it finally came out that besides the discussion of future marriage plans, there was also talk of implicit sexual activity that completely bothered Jimmy. According to Jimmy, Patty had gone up to him to share that people were saying this was going to occur as well. Patty wasn't saying she was going to do this, just that she had heard it in the rumor mill.

By the end of the conversation, parents were called and apprised of the situation and asked that they encourage their children to refrain from discussing such inappropriate topics at the school. Early adolescents seem to get involved in sexual discussions and other topics far beyond their emotional readiness to handle them. The parents assured Mrs. Lawrence that it would be handled and the rumors seemed to dissipate.

THE FIGHT

The teacher walked the two boys down to the office to see Mrs. Calhoun, the principal. She had caught the principal in the hall and shared that they were fighting on the second floor. There stood two young men who had never been in trouble for anything prior to this fight. Mrs. Calhoun wondered what caused the young men to give in to the urge to hit each other and to hit each other at school. The boys were escorted to the office, but there were so many things going on, that Mrs. Calhoun asked Tony and Fred to wait for her while she handled a few other things.

She sat them apart from each other and in plain view to make sure nothing else occurred. After around fifteen minutes, she quietly asked them to walk with her to her office in the back. They looked absolutely calm and she asked them if they had already made up, which they had. It never ceased to amaze her, but after an altercation, often they are quickly back to being friends like they used to be.

She asked them to tell her what had happened. The one young man admitted that it was really his fault, pretty unusual for a middle school student. Often they start out not telling the complete truth as they don't want to face their parents' wrath or the consequence. Tony shared that when he had arrived on campus, he noticed a binder sitting on a bench outside where he wanted to sit, so he moved it. Fred walked up and asked Tony to move, as he had saved the seat with his binder. Tony moved, not feeling great about it, but he moved.

The bell rang and they both went inside with the other students. Tony was walking down the hall and saw Fred talking with other students. Tony thought they were talking about him and what had happened and went after Fred physically, beginning to hit him on his head over and over. Fred stood there frozen, a bit shocked and didn't move. Because Fred didn't move, Tony stopped, wondering why he wasn't fighting back. The teacher then approached them and asked them to go to the office.

Mrs. Calhoun called Tony's mom and she happened to be close to the school and said she would pick him up for his suspension out of school. After mom arrived, she began to tell the principal that Tony had been having some problems with his older high school brother. His older brother had become very physical with Tony and had started to attack him. They had also discovered that his brother had been diagnosed with a psychological disorder and was now refusing to go to school. The parents were frustrated and were looking for solutions.

Their older son was also now refusing to go to school and they couldn't get him out of bed. They had called the police several times in the past and were concerned that their seventeen-year-old son was hurting their two younger sons. One never really knows what middle school students are going through or what causes them to act in certain ways while at school.

YOUR BRITCHES HAVE FALLEN DOWN!

It was time for art class to begin and Mrs. Sanchez was taking attendance. Cody, a well-mannered student who wanted to fit in, had entered the classroom, ready for class to begin. However, desiring to be a well-accepted and admired student, he took a tug at his navy blue shorts, pulling them slightly down in order to display his bright red boxer shorts. He wanted to be seen as cool and popular but didn't realize that the tug he gave brought down not only his shorts but also his boxers.

To his total embarrassment, he had mooned the entire art class, bringing about a roar of laughter and quite a reaction from the teacher. Needless to say, Cody wore his pants a bit closer to his waist from then on.

THEY WORRY AT TIMES

Mrs. Biskett, the principal, was told that a female student was crying in the clinic and couldn't stop. The principal went in to check on her. Natalia was behind the closed clinic curtain. Mrs. Biskett sat down on the clinic bed next to her and asked her what was going on. Natalia was worried as hurricane Katrina had just ripped through New Orleans. After experiencing several hurricanes in Florida the year before, it had brought back memories of what they had experienced. She had also been reading Revelations and was worried about the end times and people she knew.

Natalia opened her agenda and showed Mrs. Biskett a picture of her dad and her. She hadn't seen her dad in five years. At the time, Natalia was thirteen so this meant that she was eight years old when they had last been together. "He's an alcoholic and drug addict," she shared. Every time Natalia would call him he would rush off the phone, yet she carried his picture around every day. They continued to talk about her concerns and how she thought she could deal with them.

By the end of the conversation, Natalia was smiling. Mrs. Biskett had written down the name of a great ice cream shop that she prescribed as her "pretend doctor" (which made her smile big) for the weekend. She thought grandma would take her.

School personnel really don't know all of the worries that their students carry throughout the day. They only know about the ones that students are willing to tell them about. And they often don't find out about these until the student falls apart or begins to act out.

BITING!

Katie, one of the school's outstanding students whose grades were very high, was sent down to the office for biting another student. While middle schoolers sometimes resort to physical actions to resolve problems, biting isn't common. After sitting down to meet in his office, the principal, Mr. Shepard, asked Katie why she had decided to bite another student. Katie responded that she didn't bite him on purpose. So Mr. Shepard wondered how his arm got into Katie's mouth by mistake.

Mr. Shepard told Katie that he had never accidentally bitten anyone. She then responded, "Well, it didn't hurt [her friend] that much." When the principal told the young lady that she was going to be suspended, she told Mr. Shepard that this wouldn't work as her mother would kill her. Katie was suspended but she is still alive today.

WHAT YOU ARE TO ME!

Mr. Presley had a student in his office who was upset, but refused to talk about what was bothering him. Trey, a seventh grader, sat in his office crying, but no words would come out. After trying over and over to get him to share why he felt so badly, Mr. Presley finally asked him just to write how he felt.

Trey hesitated at first, but once he started writing, his pent up emotions began pouring out as he found the words and the courage to tell his father how upset he was with him. You see, Trey's father had recently moved out of the house, and his dad was not making much of an effort to see Trey or to communicate with him. Trey was especially angry that his father didn't take the initiative to call him and that he only returned calls when he had to.

Trey felt like his mom had become both his dad and his mom now. With the passage of time, he had started to see his dad as just another person in the world. In the letter, Trey reminded his dad that he was no longer taking on the role of a father. In fact, Trey refused to call him dad, calling him by his first name instead.

Trey was upset that his dad was using the excuse of having to work over-time, claiming that he didn't have the time to be with his son. Earning extra money wasn't everything in the world to Trey, but his relationship with his dad was. He wanted time back with his dad, but he had reached the point where he had given up on the relationship. He ended his letter by telling his dad they were just acquaintances now and that he no longer considered him his dad.

Sometimes students enter Mr. Presley's office very upset, but they are reluctant to say what is bothering them. In these cases, he often suggests that the students just write down what they are feeling. There is no pressure to share what they write. It is just meant to be a catharsis. In addition to finding relief by purging their emotions, writing also provides an avenue for students to identify more clearly what is bothering them. In Trey's case, the writing helped him find the words he needed to tell his father how he felt about their deteriorating relationship. Having found the courage to confront his father, Trey was able to move forward.

AN APOLOGY

Students often write notes apologizing to the principal. Some students are encouraged to do so by their parents, while others are self-motivated and write straight from the heart. Jack wrote a note to his principal after receiving three days of out-of-school suspension for lying to the principal. He began by thanking her for doing her job and then he asked for mercy.

He pleaded with the principal for three days of in-school suspension instead of out-of-school, begging for her to consider his request. At issue was that Jack's mother had gone down the wrong path in life due to drug use and hanging out with the wrong crowd. She had been a source of disap-pointment and grief for his grandmother and now he feared that his behavior was going to upset his grandmother. Knowing that his grandmother would be upset when she learned of his behavior at school, Jack was now requesting an in-school suspension rather than an out-of-school suspension to spare his grandmother more heartache.

Principals take these notes to heart and sometimes a different consequence is given, based on what can and should be done in order to reach the ultimate goal of changing the student's behavior in the future in a positive way.

STUCK IN THE BATHROOM

She was stuck in the bathroom and she refused to come out. The lunchroom was full of students eating and talking. Prior to the "sit in" in the girls' bathroom, Sarah had been teased by her friends that she was going out with Tim. She did not like Tim nor did she want anyone saying she was going out with him. She was humiliated. She ran to the bathroom and set up camp. No one was getting her out. She was embarrassed.

Students gathered around the bathroom but were asked to go back and sit down. Her friends were sincerely concerned about her, but now the adults at the school were trying to persuade her to come out of the bathroom. First Mr. Green, the assistant principal, sent in a girl to ask her to come out, but that didn't work. Then the female guidance counselor tried as well. No luck. She was embarrassed beyond what she could take.

Finally the lunchroom lady was able to persuade her to come out of the bathroom by gently encouraging her, saying that everything was going to be okay. Sarah quietly went back to her seat as though nothing had happened, sat down, and finished her lunch. Everyone continued to eat and the ordeal was over. Tumultuous as it seemed, things quickly resolve for the middle school student. She didn't like him and she was willing to do a "sit in" to protest the rumors. It worked.

THE SKIPPERS

Why students skip to only spend the time in the bathroom and walking the hallways is often beyond an administrator's understanding. However, two young ladies had chosen to do just this and had camped out in the bathroom. In order to amuse themselves, they had used the soap in the dispenser to decorate the mirrors. Hand prints and smears decorated all of the bathrooms mirrors and now they had become bored. They needed to do something else during their time of skipping so they decided to go for a walk. Off they went, leaving their binders on the ledge in the girls' bathroom.

When the report came to the office that the bathroom had been "decorated," Mrs. Valencia, the assistant principal, was quick to go to the bathroom in question to take pictures. She loved the challenge of figuring out who had taken on the task of redecorating the school bathroom. This investigation proved to be much easier this time.

With the help of the security cameras and the binders that were left in the bathroom, it was quickly resolved. Students in middle school seem to make decisions that do not always benefit them in the long run. They take risks and are sometimes even influenced to do something by a peer that they would not normally choose to do. Why do their peers have such an influence on them during this stage of their lives?

CAUGHT KISSING

Rita was as cute as they come! She was finishing up eighth grade and had just been called down to the principal's office to speak with her guidance counselor and principal about her kissing in the hallways. Her parents were very supportive of the school, but didn't know that she was taking on this new adventure. She bopped into the office, a huge smile on her face, knowing she couldn't be in trouble, as she had a pretty clean record.

As she learned about the phone call that was going to be made to her parents, she became a little more concerned, but still felt it would go all right. She wasn't "going out" with the young man. (Note: In middle school, when students go out, they really don't go out.) She liked him fine, but they were not dating. They just found it interesting to kiss after school if they had a chance.

After learning that dad wasn't happy at all with her, she left the office a bit more solemn. The young man's parents were called as well. No school intervention this time was done, except for the call home to the parents. Parental assistance seems to work when it comes to kissing at school.

WHY THEY DO WHAT THEY DO

This chapter contains the stuff that adolescence is made of: public embarrassment, strong emotional attachments toward parents and other caregivers, and the willingness to take risks. One of the poignant reminders about early adolescents provided by these stories is how easy it is for teens to be overwhelmed by their lives. Whether it's fighting, biting, writing (a letter to his less-than-supportive father), or hiding out in the restroom, these youngsters have encountered a fundamental fact about adolescence: the problems they encounter frequently exceed the capacity of their brains to solve them.

Public humiliation is one of their recurring fears and one of the most common problems encountered during adolescence. While some teens do everything they can to get attention, most live in fear that they will become a public spectacle. And we have all witnessed the tragic consequences among older adolescents who have become public spectacles when videos of their sexual activities are posted on social networking sites. If such publicity can provoke an older adolescent to suicide, imagine the effect that being on display has on early adolescents who don't have the skills to deal with it. Little wonder that they hide in restrooms.

A second issue that appears in this chapter is that it is during middle school that students begin to encounter adult problems. These include the traditional boy-girl problems of who likes whom and, more recently, who is having sex with whom. But they also include more serious relationship problems with family members. Take for example the boy who is convinced that his father no longer cares about him or his mother. Referring to him by name provides the son with some way of distancing himself from him and extending—on his terms—the separation that he feels he must achieve.

The tragedy here, of course, is brought into sad relief in the story of lost love, in which Natalia continues to grieve for a father whom she still loves despite the fact that he hasn't contacted her for more than five years. Inconsolable crying over a father who has not spoken to her for five years. And parents convince themselves that their kids no longer care about them and that they have no influence in their teenagers' lives!

The dilemma posed by these adult relationship problems is that teenagers are unable to solve these kinds of adult problems, both because they lack sufficient life experience and because the brain structures and processes they need for these kinds of heart-wrenching life dilemmas are simply not in place when you are in middle school. They are emerging, but it will be several more years before all the emotional and cognitive parts of the brain are connected to each other and are working well enough to solve such problems.

For example, one of the essential skills one needs to generate a solution to such complex relationship problems is the ability to focus on the problem and to inhibit one's feelings while simultaneously weighing possible solutions and considering possible outcomes. Such thinking requires brain structures and interconnections that will not finish developing until late adolescence and early adulthood. In the meantime, youngsters do the best they can with the skills they do possess.

Another important issue in this chapter is that our children really do care about the adults in their lives and they want to love and respect those adults despite all the mistakes the adults make. Do you think Trey really wanted to distance himself from his father? Given a choice, he would have chosen a close relationship.

Or, take Jack, the boy who wrote an apology to his principal pleading with her to understand his situation with his grandmother. Was Jack trying to manipulate the principal? Possibly. But what if he is sincere? The principal loses nothing by giving Jack an in-school suspension, and Jack's grandmother is spared the tribulation of yet another offspring with school problems.

Some might argue that Jack is really a con artist trying to scam his principal to avoid being punished by his grandmother. Because Jack is generally well-behaved, there is no reason to doubt his sincerity. Plus the principal will know soon enough if she is being manipulated because Jack will try it again. But all the evidence suggests that there is every reason to believe that Jack really is concerned about his grandmother's feelings and that he wants to protect his relationship with her.

The final issue that emerges from this chapter involves risk-taking and novelty-seeking. That's what "Caught Kissing" and "Skippers" are all about: the thrill derived from doing things that are new, risky, or exciting. And what could be more exciting than doing something that is prohibited by one's parents or teachers? Adolescent risk-taking is an area that has received considerable attention. This is due, at least in part, to the relationship between high-risk behaviors and accidental injuries and deaths.

As noted in chapter two, while adolescence is a time when most enjoy a prolonged period of excellent health, there is a 200 percent increase in morbidity and mortality during this same period. This dramatic increase is due in large part to accidents resulting from a combination of high-risk behaviors and poor impulse control.

Until recently, it was generally believed that higher-than-expected rates of accidental injuries and deaths were due simply to a combination of raging hormones and too little impulse control. That adolescents have too little impulse control is well documented. But the raging hormone hypothesis is not an adequate explanation for the high-risk, novelty-seeking behaviors that get teens into trouble.

The larger question, therefore, is what is the motive force that causes adolescents to engage in high-risk behaviors when they know full well that these behaviors could result in serious injuries or worse? To answer this question requires an understanding of two major brain systems: the prefrontal cortex that provides impulse control, and the limbic structures that operate the brain's reward system.

The frontal lobes of the human brain do not mature until people reach their mid- to late twenties. One effect of this is that teenagers, especially young teens, have reduced inhibition and reduced impulse control. Thus, when teens perceive the possibility of a reward, they simply can't muster a sufficient amount of impulse control to stop and consider the consequences. But diminished impulse control is only a part of the equation. To fully appreciate why teenagers pursue dangerous activities with such gusto, we need to appreciate the role of subcortical brain structures that are associated with the brain's reward system.

These structures (the amygdala, the nucleus accumbens, and the insula) go through a rapid period of growth and increased activity beginning with puberty and continuing into late adolescence, resulting in an intensification of the brain's reward system. Compared to adults, teens have more dopamine receptors, and increased receptor sites create a craving for more dopamine. Hence, teens seek out activities that result in the release of dopamine.

What kinds of activities? Mainly risk-taking and novelty-seeking, anything that is thrilling and exciting. That explains the loud music, the multitasking, the high level of physical activity, and their unending search for thrills (think roller coaster). It also explains their incessant complaints of being bored. They are seeking, seeking, seeking all the time to fill those dopamine receptors. It explains why many teenagers do things to excess. Bigger cravings lead to bigger appetites.

Contrary to popular opinion, teenagers are not simply on a quest for the riskiest, the most dangerous behaviors they can find. At the same time, they are seeking the most intense experiences they can find, which helps to explain the loud music, the fast cars, the exaggerated makeup and clothing, and the daredevil activities they engage in. These provide evidence of the early adolescent's developing brain.

By late adolescence (age eighteen or so) young people begin to show signs of restraint as dopamine cravings decline and as the inhibitory capacity of the frontal lobes matures. By our mid-twenties, the number of dopamine receptors are reduced to their normal adult range while the frontal lobes are better able to provide impulse control. The brain has, in effect, sculpted itself into its adult form, with normal adult cravings matched by the ability to exercise some degree of restraint.

Novelty-seeking and risk-taking (kissing at school, for example) stimulate the release of dopamine, the main chemical in the brain's reward system. So, when someone does something exciting (or novel or risky), the brain feels good and the person is motivated to do it again. This is especially significant for teens, because there is a rapid growth of dopamine receptors beginning in early adolescence. More receptors increase the craving for dopamine, pushing teens to seek whatever it takes to deliver more of this reward chemical.

And once the brain perceives the possibility of a reward, it is difficult for humans—and especially young teenagers—to exercise restraint. Teens are at a distinct disadvantage; as we saw earlier, the parts of the brain that provide impulse control (the frontal lobes) are not yet fully functional. When seen from this vantage point, risk-taking and novelty-seeking actually play an adaptive function.

If the frontal lobes were fully developed by age thirteen or fourteen, young teenagers might think twice about the potential negative consequences. And if they reduce risk-taking and novelty-seeking, they would stop pursuing the very activities our species uses to become self-sufficient, independent adults.

Especially after puberty, youngsters are driven by alterations in brain chemistry to take risks. If they were not driven to it, if they didn't seek what was new, if they were not willing to take risks, they would stop developing. Becoming an adult is not easy; mastering a new skill, acquiring new abilities, and forming new relationships are risky endeavors. Granted, some risky behaviors (skipping school, public displays of affection, and drinking and driving) carry the potential of significant negative consequences. But others (asking a member of the opposite sex to dance, going off to college, learning a new skill) have the potential to pay positive dividends.

The major player in all of this is the neurotransmitter, dopamine. Produced deep in the lower portions of the brain (near the cerebellum), dopamine is projected to structures in the front of the brain. These neurons have receptors that, when activated by dopamine, make us feel good.

There is also an evolutionary component to leaving home and doing risky things. Adolescents of most mammalian species are motivated to leave the hut (or nest or village) in order to increase their reproductive potential and to learn how to become self-sufficient adults. Our own young teens are not leaving the house because they don't like us. They are driven to leave the comfort of their family homes and the support of family members in exchange for the opportunity to practice the things they need to learn to become an adult.

Some of these things, such as starting their first job, are associated with positive consequences, while other adult behaviors they imitate (drinking, smoking) carry the possibility of negative consequences.

Another of these structures, the hypothalamus, produces hormones that control behaviors associated with the survival of the individual (defensive aggression) and the survival of the species (mating and care of the young). These survival instincts are strong, primeval forces that motivate us to explore the world beyond our home and family. Early adolescents, however, have little experience, knowledge, and skills to handle the potential problems that await them as they move beyond the safety of home and family. Hence, adolescent emigration is fraught with risk-taking. Becoming an adult is not going to be without some risk.

In primitive cultures, for example, adolescent boys learn the important adult skill of hunting so that they will be able to provide food for themselves and their family. In the process, the boys risk injury or even death, but benefits of self-sufficiency clearly outweigh the dangers involved. This urge to migrate has been conserved. In our own culture, teens begin a similar process of separating from their families so that they can practice adult behaviors and learn to form relationships with non-family members. Just like learning to hunt, leaving the comfort of one's home and forging new relationships also entail risk-taking.

Still not convinced? Think of the alternative to teens leaving their families. Imagine what would happen if a teenager did not feel compelled to go out into the world, to take some risks, and to try something new. That person would remain in the comfortable cocoon his or her parents provide. In fact, you probably know some folks who did just that. Didn't take risks, didn't move forward.

Chapter eight is about relationships—relationships with peers, teachers, and parents. The grand organizing relationship principle of early adolescence is that teens loosen family relationships and replace them with peer relationships. This is a normal and biologically necessary emigration, though it is difficult for parents to endure.

From the teenager's perspective, there are two problems to deal with. First, they struggle to distance themselves from their parents; second, it is difficult to form relationships with non-family members. Adolescents typically "try on" different peer relationships. However, forming and dissolving relationships is always challenging for this age group.

Establishing healthy non-family relationships is a beneficial and necessary process as it teaches youngsters how to make their way in the world. At the same time, the need to affiliate and the desire to distance themselves from family cause some children to join gangs. For others, the need for affiliation leads to "group think," in which the need to belong overwhelms their judgment. In some cases, adolescents might even relinquish their own values and engage in activities within the group that they would never do on their own.

Chapter 9

The Gifted Teen's Adventurous Nature

IS IT REALLY NECESSARY?

It was lunchtime and the eighth graders were busy socializing while eating their lunch. The lunchroom was packed full of students who were enjoying each other other's company while catching up on the latest middle school news. The administration were talking together at the far end of the cafeteria when Mr. Campbell, the principal, stopped and observed Gretchen, one of their gifted students, acting oddly at her table at the far side of the cafeteria. He wondered what she was doing.

From the distance, he saw her take something out of a Styrofoam cup, put her head way back so that her face was parallel to the ceiling, and slowly but carefully, the young lady would drop the object into her mouth. A wiggle of the neck would follow and then the procedure occurred again. The principal watched it happen around five times, asking the assistant principal if she had any idea what the student was doing. He couldn't take it any longer and quickly walked over to Gretchen to ask her about her unusual behavior.

"What are you doing?" he asked as he arrived at her table.

She quickly responded with a grin and a giggle, "I'm doing an experiment. I want to know if I can swallow my food without chewing it first and it's working!" Now this was one of their very brightest students, a real star in the school. Why would she take this chance, in order to be so inquisitive about her anatomy and study chewing like this?

Mr. Campbell insisted that she use the teeth that she was endowed with and that he didn't really want to have to administer the Heimlich on her. She needed to begin to chew right away. She giggled and responded favorably that she understood. Why do such bright young people take risks like this?

THE CHALLENGE

Four gifted eighth grade boys who were ready to move on to high school felt the need to challenge their middle school principal by making it known that they would be "disappearing" every once in a while for around ten to fifteen minutes on the campus. This "disappearing act" usually occurred during physical education class and sometimes during time spent in the media center.

Mr. Bentley wasn't quite sure what to make of their adventurous spirit and decided to not make a big deal of it although it was a concern. It had happened twice and that was enough. After the second time, he had put the teachers on alert and even asked that they keep their cars locked during the day to prevent the boys from hiding there.

One day the air conditioning went out and when the county maintenance worker showed up to repair the air conditioning unit, he discovered a stash of snacks located up in the mechanical level where a cat walk was located. He reported what he had discovered to the principal and Mr. Bentley was then ready to catch the boys in action. He believed that this had to be where the boys were hiding. Mr. Bentley set up shop in the teacher's room where the emergency ladder to the air conditioning units was located, and waited. Time went on until the missing youngsters came down the stairs to find their principal anxiously waiting for their arrival.

After the parent phone calls and their open discussion with the principal, it was discovered that the boys had been sitting up on the roof top, actually laughing at the adults as they roamed the campus looking for them. The boys had spent time watching the teacher to see when she would be out of her classroom so they could determine the exact time they could make their climb up to the upper level in order to access the school roof.

FREE, PLEASE TAKE ONE!

Eighth grade lunch had just finished and all of the students were walking back to class. Craig, a gifted student who was popular and well respected by his peers, had decided to try to make his friends laugh by standing beside a sign that had originally been placed at the school store counter in order to give away free pencils. The pencils were gone, but the sign was still there. He positioned himself beside the arrowed sign that pointed directly at him. There he stood, grin on his face, while the eighth graders walked by on their way to class. Little did he know that the principal would be walking down the same hallway with the eighth graders.

The sign read "Free, Please Take One!" and was pointing at him. The principal laughed as she went by and told him to come back from around the counter and get to class. He knew he would get a response out of it and relished the commotion he caused.

THE ALLIANCE

They were an oddly matched pair of eighth grade boys who seemed to stick together primarily because of their unusual interests and unorthodox behavior. They were not comfortable eating in the lunchroom during eighth grade lunch as they just didn't seem to mingle well with the other students. They certainly walked to the beat of a different drummer. Both boys wore wire-rimmed glasses, one was very tall, the other short, but both had a common interest in the Internet and both were academically gifted.

Instead of eating in the lunchroom, they had persuaded a new teacher on campus to work with them and allow them to eat lunch in her room. They had chosen this specific room, due to the nature of the classroom—a computer lab, where access to the Internet was easily accessible. Lunch in Mrs. Palender's room was a delight for them as they enjoyed time on the computer as well as eating, until the day the principal found out about the unusual arrangement.

After discovering what was happening, the administrator agreed to the possibility of continuing this activity, but asked that there be a signed note from the teacher stating this was going to continue on a daily basis. The office needed to know where the students were going to be every day. This was done and all went smoothly until several weeks later when the pair decided things had to change.

The duo promptly walked down to the office to meet with the principal. Why had the contract, as they called it, been violated? According to "clause two" of the contract, they were the only ones that were to eat in the teacher's classroom. However, four new students had now joined the group and were eating in the room as well. The two young men went on to explain that in addition to breaking clause two of their contract, adding these additional students would definitely take away from their collaboration time and their privacy. They insisted something had to be done!

There was actually no "contract" as they called it nor a "clause two," but the two young men were adamant that things had to change according to the agreed-upon signed document. They demanded a copy of the contract from the principal. With no contract in place, but only a signed permission note from the teacher, it was hard to comply with their demands. Keeping a serious face, but enjoying the unusual moment, the administrator shared that there was no legal document that had been breached.

I NEED SOME MONEY, MOM

Within the span of an hour, two parents called to inquire about the cost of special activities that were occurring at the school. The first mom had called to ask the cost of the field trip to Disney World. The chorus and strings students were headed for Disney World to perform. The secretary called down the music room to learn that it was twenty dollars. She then got back on the telephone and shared with the mom that it was twenty dollars. The mom gasped and exclaimed, "I'm so glad I called you! He told me it was a hundred and fifty dollars!"

Shortly thereafter, another mom called the school to ask about the Holocaust speaker who was presenting to the sixth graders that day. She had been told by her son that it was costing each student two dollars and she wanted to be sure he had it. Sad thing: there was no charge. Creative, aren't they?

WHY THEY DO WHAT THEY DO

Students with the good fortune to have been endowed with abundant academic talent are just as likely as all other teens to engage in the typical behaviors we associate with adolescence. The only difference is that they bring additional cognitive abilities to adolescent misadventures. We also see that despite superior cognitive abilities, these students make many of the same mistakes as their schoolmates. Apparently superior cognitive abilities do not inoculate them from the urges other parts of their brains are feeling. Nor does it compensate for the 20 percent of the brain that hasn't finished developing.

Take, for example, the girl trying to swallow without chewing. Her superior cognitive abilities provided her with the wherewithal to design a science experiment. If you have a question, you generate a hypothesis, and then test the hypothesis. But why in the lunchroom where other students can ridicule you and the administration can observe you? Because, as we saw in the last chapter, once teens get something in their head, it is difficult not to act on it. Then what about the potential choking hazard? Well, that's a potential consequence, and teens, even smart ones, don't usually consider the consequences of their behavior.

In "The Challenge" and in "I Need Some Money, Mom" we again see the immature adolescent brain completely overwhelm the boys' superior cognitive abilities. You see, the boys' superior cognition reflects the functional capacity of the cortex. As noted earlier, the cortex consists of six layers of cells that are responsible for movement, information processing, and a range of cognitive and academic abilities. But just underneath this three-millimeter covering are the brain's emotion-generating structures, and they are just dying to get out.

This collection of structures, known collectively as the limbic system, is where the gremlins live. And, just like in the movie, the gremlins are always trying to escape so that they can cause havoc. Some gremlins are just mischief makers (a practical joke, mild teasing), but other gremlins can be downright mean (temper tantrums, aggression toward others, loss of self-control). At worst, you might even think of the gremlins as the seven deadly sins (pride, envy, gluttony, greed, lust, anger, sloth). In older adolescents and adults, the gremlins are kept in their places because the frontal lobes keep them there. Not so with teenagers, especially young ones.

But every once in a while, the emotional parts of our brains overwhelm our frontal lobes and the gremlins are set free. When that happens, a person's emotions get expressed. The boys on the roof and the boys asking for money when it wasn't needed are examples of mischief-making gremlins at work. The boys on the roof just wanted to have fun. Because of their cognitive abilities, they are able to hatch a detailed plan that included careful planning and precise timing. This is a testament to their cognitive abilities.

And what of the risk of getting caught? Like all other teens, the boys on the roof and the boys seeking money either didn't think about getting caught or they were willing to take the risk. In the case of highly intelligent teenagers, it is a good bet that they considered the consequences and that any potential risks were well worth the thrill of matching wits with their adult supervisors.

And what of the boys having lunch in the classroom who want to pit their emerging concept of justice and fair play against that of the adults? Well, first, they really wanted to be left alone during lunch and that urge motivated them to seek asylum in a teacher's classroom and to protect what they considered their space. This is a case of reward seeking.

But then why challenge the decision to allow other students in the room? Because teens practice being adults. And one of the things adults do is to argue in court. So these boys want to practice that adult behavior to see if they can do it. It is up to the principal to decide if he wants to view their legalistic approach as a challenge to his authority or simply two teens practicing an adult role.

And what of the boy holding the sign? He is simply having a dopamine moment. He needed a little reward (in the form of attention), probably because he was getting bored and needed a little pick-me-up, something to keep him going through the afternoon. He's a smart kid, so he knows enough not to do something that will get him into trouble, but that will satisfy his cravings and increase his arousal.

The bottom line with gifted students: they will be more creative, more thoughtful, and more mindful. But their superior cognitive abilities simply make their antics more interesting. And antics they will have, because their frontal lobes are still immature and dopamine and other neurochemicals are still being released.

Chapter 10

Academic Challenges

RIGHT-LEG ANSWERS

Susie was a great student, but she had not studied for the science exam. She had worked very hard to come up with a plan to keep her parents happy with a satisfactory grade but at the same time not spend too much of her time studying. Early in the morning, before school, she borrowed a marker from another student and quickly wrote the answers from her study sheet on her right thigh, where her skirt would cover the writing. She was confident the plan would go off without a hitch and all would be good.

After entering Mrs. Sink's classroom, she carefully positioned herself in the chair, with her skirt strategically placed, ready to be raised on her leg enough to show the answers and then cover them up again. One answer completed and it was working well! Another one, still not noticed and all was good. However, her teacher noticed the repetitive motions and closely observed Susie in her subversive actions.

Walking slowly over to the young lady, Mrs. Sink lowered her head close to Susie's and instructed her to go to the restroom to wash off the answers on her leg. She was caught; Mrs. Sink was on to her shrewd plan. On her way to the bathroom, she couldn't believe she had been caught. She finally arrived at the sink and began to scrub and scrub, and then furiously scrub some more. The writing was not coming off!

When her leg turned red and became painful she finally gave up, realizing at that moment that the marker she had borrowed was a permanent marker. Red leg and answers still on her leg, she walked back to the classroom to share her failed attempt of washing it off. She had learned her lesson, the hard way.

SOMETIMES YOU JUST NEED TO SEW

Johnny had a meltdown in class. He couldn't sew and that's all there was to it. Out of anger and frustration, he had lost it crying in the middle of the class while everyone was busy working on their own piece of the quilt. He was embarrassed and he just needed to leave the room. As quickly as possible he was sent to the main office to find someone to console him.

The social studies class had been studying the Underground Railroad and had learned about the quilts that had been made and hung on clotheslines for the runaway slaves. Slaves that were running for freedom would find the quilts which had secret codes on them that told where they could go next in order to find shelter and food on their journey to freedom.

As part of a culminating activity, the eighth graders were constructing a quilt and learning in the process how to sew. Johnny, a gifted student, was frustrated with the task and had about as much as he could take. Off he went to the principal's office to talk it out. When he entered her office, Mrs. Gordon sat and listened to Johnny as he told of his struggle with the class that day. After several minutes, Mrs. Gordon asked if she could retrieve the sewing project that he had left in the class and assist him with it. Gordon agreed that might be a good idea and the sewing began.

Up and down, making a knot, and placing the fabric pieces in just the right spot soon seemed secondary as they discussed what really was bothering Johnny. He was worried about his grades. He had wanted to go to college, but after he entered sixth grade, he believed that he wasn't smart enough for it, even though he was gifted. He would do fine at the beginning of each year, then slack off and earn some F's, and then have to get stressed out to bring the grades back up. If he didn't complete this sewing project, he was worried that he wouldn't make the grade he needed.

As they sewed and talked, it was obvious that Johnny just needed to talk. This project had become the last straw for him. As he talked with the principal he realized again that it was just for a completion grade. Plans for college and his future were discussed as the sewing went on. He missed jazz band that day, but he had sat and sewed with the principal, and he needed it that day. Some days you just need to sew.

RICKY AND HIS FACTS

Ricky was a great young man and had a great future to look forward to. He was one of the oldest boys in the eighth grade. He was polite, well-mannered, and academically focused. The only struggle that Ricky had was memorizing his multiplication facts. He had just gotten his driver's license and was really excited about going to high school. Not knowing his facts really bothered him though and he had discussed this frustration with his math teacher.

Mrs. Bramble, the math teacher, eventually went to the principal out of concern about Ricky's inability to memorize all of his facts. He knew some of them, but didn't seem to be able to memorize all of them. The eighth grade math class was well beyond learning their multiplication facts so Mrs. Bramble was hoping that they could find a tutor for Ricky.

The day of the meeting, the principal, Mr. Samuel, decided to take on the task and started meeting on a daily basis with Ricky to work on the facts. It might only take fifteen minutes each day, but this was something he really wanted to do in order to make a difference in this young man's life. Together they eventually began to master all of the facts; however, it took creativity.

Mr. Samuel discovered that Ricky needed to visualize the concepts so he could recall the facts later. The principal began drawing pictures of various objects with the math facts in the picture. For instance, a 3 × 3 would be a picture of a tree with the 9 as the trunk. Mr. Samuel would bring up the tree and then Ricky would remember the answer as 9. Why is it harder for some students to memorize their multiplication facts than for others?

THEY FEEL FOR THEIR PARENTS' WORRIES

Students so often take on the blame for their parents getting a divorce, worry excessively about their parents' financial woes, or become excessively involved in an older sibling's behavioral issues. They might feel that their parents argued because of them or that the parents would not have fought so badly if only they had been home. Owning into their families' hardships often brings about lower grades and the onset of depression within middle school students. They feel for their parents and have a hard time staying out of the center of the stressful situations.

With the onset of anxiety and/or depression come low grades for a season. It is one of the first signs that teachers see. Guidance counselors are notified, so they can create a plan to monitor the student's grades until they improve. Often an outside counselor is also recommended to the parent in order to bring about a speedy recovery.

It is to be expected that students will feel the stress at home. With the middle school hormonal changes going on, these times of stress can also be exaggerated and need extra attention in order to get the students through the hard times they are facing. Working hand in hand with a counseling agency or the local guidance counselor, the students' grades usually begin to rise as students develop coping strategies and time goes on.

YOU'RE EMBARRASSING ME!

Tirelessly Mom had come in for the third conference with the team of eighth grade teachers about her son's continued lack of academic success. The teachers discussed their concerns with the mother and again reviewed the lack of motivation that they were seeing on the young man's part. They felt like they had tried everything in order to get him motivated, but nothing seemed to help in getting him to do his classwork and homework in a timely fashion or to even get it turned in at all.

The young man's mother was desperate. She was at her wit's end after visiting with the teachers for the third time that school year with no improvement from her son. All of a sudden it hit her, to the surprise of the teachers and the young eighth grader. Mom stood up and announced, "You've embarrassed me long enough! Now I'm going to embarrass you."

The bell rang outside the classroom door; she stood up, promptly took the back of her long hair and flopped it over her face so as to not show her face. She grabbed her son's hand and proceeded through the hallway with her hair in her face and holding tightly to her son's hand. They received quite a bit of attention from his classmates as they progressed through the halls!

Due to her promise to repeat this unusual display if his grades did not improve, she never had to worry about it again. He immediately began working the next day and moved on to high school with flying colors. Not to say that this was a model of what should be done, but it does appear that it takes a motivating factor to sometimes spur a middle schooler to do what should be done in the first place. The teachers continue to smile about the day they watched a middle schooler leave the school holding hands with his mom with her hair-covered face.

WHY SHOULD I DO THE WORK?

She was kind, beautiful, and usually a high-achieving eighth grader who had decided she didn't feel like it was important to get her school work done. During the fall semester, her grades had been good. However, during the third nine-week grading period, she had let her work slide even more and now had earned several D's and F's. She, however, was satisfied with her grades and felt like she could coast through the rest of the year because she had earned A's and B's in the fall semester.

As part of her daily schedule, she attended a research class in which students studied various environmental issues. Her research project involved the channeled apple snails that had invaded the local lakes. However, when she discovered that she wasn't going to be chosen to present her research on an out-of-town field trip, she was devastated. Sarah went to her teacher and asked what she could do. She was told that if she went to her other teachers and tried to raise her grades by asking for makeup work, she could then apply to go on the field trip and represent the school for the competition out of town.

Sarah worked extremely hard to achieve her goal and eventually persuaded her teachers, some who did not usually take late work, to assist her with her goal. Due to her new motivation and incentive, Sarah spent hours working to raise her grades. She was able to do just that and brought the grades up to A's and B's within the nine-week period. Her teacher was impressed and Sarah went on the trip, presenting what they had learned about channeled apple snails and their impact on the city's lakes.

Finding a motivating factor will assist students with raising their grades when they are low. Something has to jump start them to motivate them enough to make the change and value good grades. They need to see the reason for doing well in school. How do we find these "triggers" that will motivate them to perform at their highest capability?

WHY THEY DO WHAT THEY DO

The permanent marker story is priceless; it contains just about every element of the adolescent journey. First, there is the decision to cheat. Talk about identity formation!! Here is an otherwise successful student who—to avoid embarrassment and to keep up her grade point average—tries on a new role to see how it fits. Then her brain takes over, or should we say her brain starts to get in the way, as she forgets to see if it is a permanent marker.

As we have seen, she is smart in school, but not smart in life. Life is different. She didn't study permanent versus dry erase markers, so it is not on her radar screen. And when she decided that a little mild cheating would get her needs met, the possibility of anything bad happening simply disappeared.

The sewing story brings up a very important aspect of adolescent development. Clearly, Johnny's problem was not sewing. But had his teacher and principal treated his outburst as unruly behavior, they would have forfeited the opportunity to provide this frightened young man what he really needed. Middle schoolers don't yet possess the problem-solving skills to match the obstacles they encounter. Johnny is a perfect example of that.

In the first place, he regularly digs himself into a hole because he fails to anticipate the consequences of not doing his work. Then he starts to panic, his arousal increases, and he gets overwhelmed by his emotions. We know that adolescence places children at increased risk for all sorts of problems. And one of the best antidotes for saving teenagers from these dangers is a relationship with caring adults.

The second thing the talk provided Johnny was the opportunity to identify his real problem and to begin solving it. We need to remember that early teenagers don't think well; if they can't remember that there is a camera in the hall, can we expect them to reason through this college problem? It's not their fault, of course. It's just that their brains are getting in the way. In the meantime, it helps immensely if adults provide the time and circumstances for them to learn the problem-solving skills they need to tackle adult problems.

Participating in sports can also provide an important protective mechanism. In addition to satisfying their thrill-seeking urges, sports impose a routine on a teenager's schedule. But the most important thing that sports provides is an adult mentor in the form of a coach who cares about the players.

Having a relationship with a caring adult may explain the results of one study that showed that while 50 percent of girls not participating in athletics had become sexually active, fewer than 21 percent of girls on athletic teams had had sex.[11] On a similar note, one has to wonder whether it was visualization or the care and attention of the principal/tutor that was instrumental in Ricky learning the multiplication tables.

But what about the mom who decided that her Cousin It (a character on the TV series, *The Adams Family,* whose hair covered his face) routine was a reasonable intervention for her son's lackadaisical attitude toward his studies? Though we can't know her background in adolescent development, she capitalized on an essential truth about teenagers: that they will do just about anything—even their school work—to avoid being publicly embarrassed.

While most teens seek attention and affirmation, they want it on their terms. For example, eating a frog heart in front of several hundred students is a reputation maker. Being seen in public with Cousin It is a reputation buster. Better to do your school work.

It's the same with Sarah. As long as it met her needs to let her grades slide, she let her grades slide. But once she became aware of the consequences of low performance, she began to turn things around. Unfortunately, she was unable to see this consequence on her own. It needed to hit her over the head. Sarah teaches us an important lesson, that while getting needs met can lead teens into some very negative situations, getting their needs met can also lead teens in some very positive directions. It is important to remember that the motivation they feel is not just negative.

Risk-taking, novelty-seeking, and impulsivity are the hallmarks of adolescence. We generally think of these as being negative, as the things that lead teens to drug use, driving while intoxicated, and unprotected sex. But we need to remember that there is more than a little risk-taking in asking someone to dance, in asking someone on a date, and in trying to get better at sports, art, music, or school.

Likewise, it is novelty-seeking that propels us from the security of childhood to take on the challenges of adulthood. Even impulsivity has its advantages. If you didn't act on impulse, you might never get up and try anything. The things that get teens into trouble are the very same things that they use to become adults. We can't have it both ways.

Academic performance is one of those areas in which identity formation plays itself out. The teenager's job is school, and they are encouraged by parents and teachers to do this job well. However, maintaining high academic achievement requires persistence, planning, and endurance. It also demands giving up immediate rewards for long-term consequences. These are not qualities that most teenagers come by easily.

While parents and teachers are all encouraging students to work harder, the students are struggling with identity formation. The irony is that while adults argue that students just need to work harder, students equate high performance with being smart, not working hard. If young adolescents do not identify themselves as being smart, they don't see any point in trying to get an A. Where adults need to apply their efforts is in helping their children understand the relationship between hard work and high achievement. It's doing your homework every day that will lead to achievement, not that you are just smart.

Chapter 11

Socially They Struggle at Times

HE'S ANGRY AGAIN

Sam was a tough cookie and proud of it. No one was going to go against him or he would share his mind with them. He had worked hard to develop this reputation. On this particular day, teachers sent six students to the office to wait for the principal because they were not in proper attire according to the school's policies. When Mrs. Slopane arrived at the main office after morning duty, four students were there and two were "missing in action," including Sam, the tough cookie.

Mrs. Slopane asked someone in the office to call Sam and his friend down to the office while she dealt with the four compliant students. They quickly discussed the clothing concerns and away they went. Finally, the other two students arrived. One of the young men, very remorseful that he had left the office without permission, received only a stern warning. Then it was Sam's turn. Sam began to display his usual mannerisms by reacting with an inappropriate attitude and tone of voice.

Over the years, the principal had learned that Sam's dad often argued with him and they yelled at each other regularly. The prior year, Mrs. Slopane had asked Sam to try remaining calm with his dad to see if this would calm his dad down. The next year, during one of his episodes he shared with the principal that it didn't work. He informed Mrs. Slopane that "he needed to handle it and had to start yelling again at his dad."

Mrs. Slopane asked him to sit in the other end of the office until he could discuss the situation with her in a calm and respectful manner. After about twenty minutes he was ready.

They talked about Sam's future and what would happen if he displayed this type of behavior on the job. He knew the right answers but they continued to have this behavior throughout the years.

UTTER DISTURBANCE

Sammy felt pretty distressed about what he had done. He had been taught he needed to concentrate on getting a good education in order to be successful in life. At times, however, he just didn't get along with others. He composed a note to his principal apologizing for the disturbance he had created due to fighting at school.

Sammy began with an apology, giving the date of the fight and the location. He then went on to explain that his goal was to attend the University of South Carolina and he knew that acting in the way that he did might jeopardize his chances of being accepted at USC. He asked for forgiveness and he promised that this would never occur again.

FORGIVENESS

The students were having a lively discussion in their language arts class on forgiveness when reflecting on "A Retrieved Reformation" by O. Henry. The girls began by saying that everyone knows that after an argument girls, as a group, give hugs and tell each other that "everything is okay now." There is a lot of emotion and many tears, but the girls soon get over it and are friends again.

They observed though that guys, on the other hand, were a tougher breed. One of the young seventh grade boys, Scott, shouted out, "Guys forgive like this!" and spontaneously slapped another boy across the face. Not knowing that the slap would sound so loud, it shocked Scott. The entire class exploded into laugher over the Scott's decision and the difference between the boys and the girls. Teens make impulsive decisions and their social skills are sometimes lacking. Knowing how to deal with each other in an appropriate manner doesn't come easily!

GUYS HANDLE IT DIFFERENTLY

Three young sixth graders who had never been to the office before were quickly ushered to the assistant principal's office to discuss what had just happened. All three of them looked a bit shocked about all of the commotion made over what they had just done. Their pale but blushing faces told the story of embarrassment, surprise, and worry about how their parents were going to react once they heard the news. Each student was asked to write down what had happened.

George's version:

Alex pushed me with his tummy into Joey who yelled "who did that!?!?!" And I was all like—Alex did it! Joey yelled at Alex, "What's your problem?" Alex did not respond but instead angrily book dropped Joey. Alex attempted to run off but super-fast Joey jumped on him and got him into a head lock. Alex spun him around and threw him down furiously. Then both stared at each other seriously and both ran off to class. That is how it happened.

Alex's version:

George told me that I went to counseling and I pushed him against Joey and walked out. Joey called me a retard and I book dropped him and ran away he then chased after me and jumped on my back and grabbed around my neck and I picked him up and dropped him on his back.

Joey's version:

I was leaving the lunchroom as George is getting rammed against the door by Alex and I tell him not to do it again and he bookdrops me and I run after him, jump on his back telling him not to do it again and I get flipped over his back. I get up like nothing and I'm about to punch him but he gets away and I start to go for him, but decide to cool down and go to class.

Middle school boys tend to want to handle their aggressive feelings physically, without thinking about the consequences of their actions. It happens without much forethought and it is over when it is over.

THE LONERS

Every school year, Mrs. Grace noticed that there would be a few "loners" that would not have many friends at their lunch table. They would often have a book, would eat quietly from a lunch brought from home, glasses on their faces, and would stare into the book while they ate. These students preferred it like this; they didn't want to socialize. They didn't want to hear the news from others. Just give them a book and their lunch box and they were happy.

The other middle schoolers leave them alone as well and do not question this behavior. It is an unspoken tale of a few middle schoolers every school year. Their grades are good; their behavior in class is acceptable, although, once in a while the book is taken away as the student reads instead of doing the assignment.

What causes some of our youth to prefer to be in another world? There are just a few, but they stand out in the crowd as the few that want to be left alone, in their own preferred setting while reading about another world.

GIRL DRAMA

Girl drama seemed to be at the top of the list of "things to do" for Mrs. Jones, the principal. She actually kept a large basket of science toys on her conference table in order to have them available when the drama was discussed in her office. The disagreement often seemed to be based on whether one girl liked a boy and if the other one was now stepping in or if people were saying they were "going out" when they really weren't "going out."

This time it involved a birthday party at a popular girl's house that the students had attended over the weekend. However, one of the girl's boyfriends had texted another girl at the party. When the text was discovered and floated around the party atmosphere, feelings were in an uproar! How dare her friend actually text her boyfriend back! However, none of the girls seemed to blame the boyfriend for starting the problem by texting a friend of his girlfriend.

The social chat rooms were filled with students' comments and by the time Monday rolled around, it was all over the seventh grade hallways that the girls were going to fight. Mrs. Jones was immediately told about the rumors and was quick to call the girls down to her office for their opportunity to verbally confront each other.

It always took some time to work through the situation, but as soon as it was over, the girls were out the door to announce it to the world. They had quickly made up and were ready for new girl drama. Why do they involve themselves in the drama and why is it usually among friends? Why do they never hold the boys accountable for their actions?

WHY THEY DO WHAT THEY DO

Often, it seems, adolescence is defined as a time of difficult social relationships. When people look back at their own teenage years, they recall struggling with their parents over house rules, curfews, food choices, allowances, and choice of friends. Others have painful memories of being mistreated, teased, and ostracized by others. The transition from childhood to adulthood is not easy, and difficulties in managing social relationships with individuals outside one's family pose major challenges.

One of the recurring criticisms of teenagers is that they are cruel to each other, to siblings, and to parents and teachers. This is, after all, the time when aggressive actions reach their peak. Recall from chapter 2 that the 200 percent increase in death and injury during this time is due to accidents, homicides, and suicides, much of which comes in the form of antisocial and aggressive behavior. Think about it: peer-to-peer fighting is virtually absent in most elementary schools, yet it is a common occurrence in most middle schools.

There is an important point to make here. First, as discussed before, the overwhelming majority of teens (80–90 percent) do not fight, they don't commit murder, and they are not self-destructive. As with adults, most violent acts are committed by a very tiny portion of the total population. But while most adolescents do not solve their social problems in aggressive and antisocial ways, the vast majority of adolescents stumble into a host of social interaction challenges following puberty.

Because social problems and puberty happen to coincide it was generally believed that social problems were due to hormonal imbalances. To some extent, this is true, but as with so much about early adolescence, hormonal changes alone do not provide a sufficient explanation for the social upheavals that characterize this developmental stage. The social problems adolescents encounter can be traced to two sources: brain changes (including structural and neurochemical changes) and external pressures related to relationships with parents and relationships with peers.

As noted in previous chapters, there is a natural tendency for post-pubertal children to begin to migrate away from their family and to spend more time in the company of peers. From an evolutionary standpoint, emigration serves an adaptive function. Moving away helps to ensure that reproductive activity occurs a safe distance from consanguineous relatives, thereby protecting the gene pool.

In our culture, adolescents tend to remain a part of their family of origin long past puberty. Nevertheless, there are strict legal, religious, and cultural taboos that prohibit consanguineous relationships, and there remains this urge for adolescents to seek more independence and to separate from their family.

When children seek more privileges and more independence than parents are willing to give, conflicts arise. When this occurs (and it occurs in most families) it is time to renegotiate and redefine the parent-child relationship. Unfortunately, what occurs in many families is a long and protracted battle over who the decision maker will be.

But during the arguments, a second problem is encountered. The little darling who accepted on faith all (at least most) of what her parents said now begins to challenge their decisions and opinions. Although most parents are shocked and offended by this sudden change, it is important to keep in mind that after puberty, there is an increase in cognitive development that results in teens being able to think for themselves, to form their own opinions, and to question the opinions of others.

While most parents insist that they want their children to develop these traits, most recoil when their children employ them at home. Yes, parents want children who think for themselves and who are not afraid to challenge the views of others. It's just that they are surprised when their children display these traits at home or in school.

As teens venture into the world of their peers, they inevitably encounter relationship problems with each other. One of the first steps in moving from family to peers is finding peers with similar interests, tastes, and values. Once they find a group and they are accepted, they quickly adopt the language, the dress, and the customs of their peer group. This process of socialization is strongest during the middle school years when teenagers are just beginning to separate from parents and are in a hurry to find a substitute for the concern and support that the family provided.

Choosing a peer group is a crucial step in identity formation, but peer group selection and socialization carry the seeds of conflict as groups compete with each other for status. The most obvious and tragic example of peer group conflict is gang warfare, where large amounts of drug money and access to firearms has created a deadly culture of allegiance and revenge. Though not nearly as deadly, peer group rivalries are played out in dozens of ways every day.

The aggressive tendencies that impel teens to compete with each other are thought to be fueled by estrogen and testosterone. But it is not just the presence of these hormones that is creating the problems. They have been present since birth (and before), but the brain has managed to maintain normal levels of these hormones during childhood.[12]

With the onset of puberty, however, two important changes occur in the brain. The first is that overproduction of receptor sites that the hormones attach to and activate. As noted earlier, some of these will die off (pruning). Second, there are sudden fluctuations in the production of sex hormones. It is not that teens have too much of these gonadal hormones. Rather, it is the abrupt changes in hormone levels that contribute to teenagers' exaggerated emotional responses, unexplained mood swings, irritability, and aggressive reactions.

In boys, these aggressive tendencies tend to be expressed physically. Differences are settled quickly and decisively with a clear winner and a clear loser. Males then move on with this new (or reconfirmed) social hierarchy in place. Although physical fights among girls are increasing, girls tend to engage in relational aggression. Whereas boys elevate their status with physical prowess, girls do so by damaging the status and established relationships of other girls they see as rivals.[13] Along with cyber-bullying, relational aggression has been enhanced and made easier with the appearance of social networking sites.

But these interpersonal problems are not solely a function of fluctuating levels of sex hormones. There is also a rapid release of oxytocin (dubbed the prosocial hormone, because of its effects on feelings of attraction toward and caring for others) and an increase in cortisol, the stress hormone. As much as the sex hormones, stress hormones contribute to adolescent irritability and to periodic outbursts of verbal and physical aggression. Again, it is not the presence of these hormones that are the problem for adolescents; rather, it is the fluctuations (too much, then too little) of these hormones that create interpersonal problems for teenagers.

To make matters worse, one very crucial social skill actually declines during adolescence.

First of all, face recognition declines between ages eleven and fourteen. Except for social embarrassment, this temporary loss poses few significant problems. However, early adolescents experience a mild to moderate decline in the ability to process emotional, stressful, or anxiety-provoking stimuli in the facial expressions of others. If adults are puzzled by the seemingly bizarre and aggressive responses of teenagers, it is worth remembering that, no, they might not see that you are sad, or angry, or hurt, because their brains don't interpret facial expressions very well and that is how we express our feelings.

Charles Darwin wrote about this in a book entitled *The Expression of Emotion in Animals and Man*. During his famous voyage on the HMS *Beagle*, he discovered that the expression of emotions is similar in humans across regions and across cultures. All people smile when they are happy. These are not learned responses. They seem to be innate. And the ability to read the expression of emotions on other people's faces accurately is essential for responding appropriately to the emotions of others. Being unable to do so puts one at a distinct disadvantage.

There is one additional comment about peer relationships that is worth noting. As children transition from elementary school to middle school and from middle school to high school, parents often worry that their children will be influenced negatively by peer pressure. To be sure, peer pressure exerts an increasing influence as children get older.

In elementary school, children tend to spend more time with family and family influences dominate. Beginning in late childhood and early adolescence, however, children spend increasing amounts of time with peers, with a corresponding rise in peer influence. In fact, during a typical school day, adolescents spend four times more time with peers than they do with parents. Not surprisingly, peer influences begin to make inroads.

But before you try to shield your child from outside influences, there are several things to keep in mind. Once children reach puberty, structural and chemical changes in their brains combined with a lack of impulse control, lead to novelty-seeking and risk-taking. Like it or not, they are going to try on new things as they seek to define who they are and who they want to be. And because they are now spending more time with peers, the advice and consent of peers generally carries more weight than that of their parents. To develop their own identity, they must separate from their parents. But they do so with the support of their peer group.

And for the overwhelming majority of early adolescents, their peer group consists of youngsters with similar interests and backgrounds. Kids tend to form cliques and cliques tend to be segregated along racial, cultural, religious, and socioeconomic lines. That the peer group replaces the family is not necessarily a bad thing, because the peer group provides boundaries that keep young teens contained. Without the constraining influence of the peer group, there is no telling where untethered, novelty-seeking teens might roam in search of their own identity.   Finally, peer groups don't find individuals; individuals find peer groups. And by and large, teenagers choose groups that are composed of kids with similar tastes, interests, and values. If your teen hangs out with high-achieving students, chances are very good that your teen is a high-achieving student. Likewise, if you child begins to affiliate with drug users, chances are very good that your child is a drug user. They are not seduced into drug use by peers, any more than non-athletes are seduced into sports by peers. Drug users find other drug users, just as athletes find other athletes.

Chapter 12

Emotional Episodes and Psychological Concerns

THE INTERNET ACQUAINTANCE WAS
READY TO PICK HER UP

When Mr. Miller, the administrator in charge, heard that a young man had driven from Kentucky to pick up one of the students from his Florida middle school, he was quick to react. He had been told that Rachel, a popular eighth grader in the school, was up on the second story of the school crying about this seventeen-year-old Internet friend that had showed up at her school to pick her up from out of state. Several friends had circled around the young lady to encourage and console her while others had run down to the office to report what they had heard.

Outside in the car rider line, parked out of the way, stood the seventeen-year-old young man, waiting for his Internet friend to come downstairs so they could meet. Mr. Miller approached his car and told the young man that he needed to leave the campus right away. The police had been called and he was not welcome at the school. Even though he was asked to leave, the seventeen-year-old insisted that he was supposed to pick up Rachel and that she would be expecting him. After Mr. Miller said again that this would not be happening, the young man left campus.

Although this incident ended in a positive way, it does appear that middle school youth feel that they are immune from dangerous situations. They think that things like this will not happen to them. Rachel, a National Junior Honor Society student who was well respected by the teachers and students, had made some choices that could have had very serious implications. In her innocence, she believed that the friends on the Internet were safe and assumed that she was old enough to make good choices in sharing information about herself.

Rachel's parents were notified and the seriousness of the event was discussed with their daughter. They were grateful it ended so well but also seemed a bit surprised that their daughter would share personal information with strangers on the Internet when they had been so cautious in training her on what was appropriate use of the Internet.

CUTTERS

As a principal, Mrs. McDougal had experienced the same sort of event one or two times every year: a student has numerous cuts on her arms and is hiding the one-inch carvings under long sleeves or excessive jewelry. The cuts can also be seen on her legs and the student usually says at first that a dog or cat has made the scratches. Another student usually reports the concern to the principal confidentially, worried about her friend. It seems the story is always the same.

Usually the student denies deliberately hurting herself. Then the truth comes out. The student then shares when and how it was done. These students will find a small tool to use: it might be a small piece of glass, a sharp edge, a box cutter, a broken ruler with a metal edge, or a razor. Sometimes it's a stick pin. The marks are very similar in nature and are around an inch long. The cuts are repeated over and over on the arms and legs but done in spots that can be covered and hidden from all adults.

When Mrs. McDougal calls the parents, they usually aren't aware that the cutting is occurring. She tells them that according to their child, this has been done in the son's or daughter's bedroom at night in the dark or behind the house in a secretive place. Mrs. McDougal has never really been given a strong reason as to why students do this, just that they felt sad. Whenever this happens, the school officials call the parents, document the information and suggest outside counseling. It is so sad. Why do they want to cut their bodies?

OCD

Students with obsessive-compulsive disorder (OCD) sometimes experience challenges in the academic setting; however, they can be excellent students. They can struggle with uncomfortable thoughts about a need to fix something, or with the compulsion to count something. Their thoughts move quickly and when under stress the symptoms are magnified. Some feel the need to wash their hands repeatedly while counting the times it is done before they feel it is okay to walk away.

The OCD symptoms are not constantly present, but can appear frequently throughout the day. When students with OCD are feeling more stressed than normal, the symptoms will increase in frequency until things slow down for the student. Although these students usually do really well in school, there are times that they feel or think about the need to double- or triple-check something.

Sometimes a student with OCD takes longer to complete an assignment for the teacher because he/she has to keep erasing the answers and then rewriting them in order to feel okay or in order to prevent something bad from happening.

How do we work with the students that have OCD and what is the best way to encourage them?

FOUR WEEKS OF CRYING

The guidance counselor was busy, so Lisa was hand-delivered to the principal to cry. The young sixth grader didn't know why she felt like crying; she only knew she needed to let the tears flow. And they did, for quite a long time. Mrs. Grant didn't really know how to get her to stop either. She questioned her about her classes, her grades, her home life, anything to get her to talk, but Lisa just wanted to cry.

After finally getting the tears to stop, Lisa was on her way back to class and then broke into tears again. Mrs. Grant had discovered that Lisa essentially had three parents—one stepparent and two biological parents—and she was on the move every week, taking turns living in two different homes. She also learned that Lisa's dad had lost three jobs recently and had just started another new job. Her dad's first job had been steady for ten years and so this job situation was a shock to the family.

Lisa was carrying the burden for her family and the unusual stress that was placed on her to try and please three parents, instead of just two. She wanted to please everyone and tried so hard to keep her grades up. Students seem to carry the load of what they see happening with their parents but they can't always express how worried they are.

THERE'S ALWAYS A REASON

There's always a reason for what a middle school student does, but you can't always figure it out until you delve deep. Mrs. Boone, an eighth grade teacher, ran into the cafeteria very upset with Cynthia because she had refused to take off her hat and also refused to come into the cafeteria to see the principal about it. Emotions were running high and the teacher was fed up. "Why would she defy me like this? Why won't she take off the hat? I've had it! Cynthia says that the principal has to go outside if she wants to talk to her. What is she thinking?"

Mrs. Radcliffe, the principal, sat there calmly listening to the irate teacher. She then requested that one of the lunchroom ladies ask Cynthia to come into the cafeteria to talk, informing her that she would receive an office referral if she didn't come inside. It worked. In came Cynthia, her head covered with a black woolen cap. Cynthia sat down at the table where the principal was sitting during lunch duty.

Mrs. Radcliffe looked at her thoughtfully and asked, "What's going on? Why won't you take off the hat?" Cynthia, a bit frustrated, looked at Mrs. Radcliffe and shrugged her shoulders. She had gotten into a predicament that she didn't know how to get out of.

Mrs. Radcliffe asked Cynthia to go into the cafeteria bathroom and take off her hat, check her hair and come back to the table. Cynthia sat there, looking concerned, but didn't say a word. Mrs. Radcliffe looked at her again and asked, "What's going on with your hair? Are you embarrassed?"

Cynthia looked at her and responded, "Half of my hair is in braids and the other half is not. I want to go home. Can I call my mom?"

Mrs. Radcliffe responded, "No, you can't call your mom to go home, you need to be in school and do your work. Why did you take half of your braids out?" Cynthia shrugged her shoulders again, this time with a little more humility. She was embarrassed but was not willing to let anyone know. It seemed to be preferable for her to get in trouble than to let anyone know her hair was not presentable.

The decision was made to allow her to keep her sleep bonnet (that kept her hair in place overnight) but have her sit in the office for the rest of the day to get her work done. No need to embarrass her by requiring the hat to come off, but there was a need for her to learn. There's always an underlying reason why they act the way they do.

HE WAS READY TO DEFEND THEIR HONOR

Randy, a tall, lean, and good-looking eighth grader, was escorted to the office after several girls had shared how worried they were about their friend. Randy told them he was going to 'defend their honor' by confronting another boy that he claimed posed a threat to them. He also wanted the girls to report to an adult if he didn't show up at school again. He intended to meet him after school in the bus rider loop, where the fight was to occur. He had to do it, he told the girls. He had to show them that he really cared about them.

When the school resource officer and the assistant principal called the young man down to the office, Randy was hesitant to talk about the event. He was really was surprised that the girls had told on him. For over an hour, Randy insisted that this was something he really needed to do.

Randy had made it all up in order to impress the girls and to show how much he cared for them. He wanted to be seen as a hero in their eyes. Of course, the girls found out that Randy made up the whole story. Things didn't work out like he had planned. Why do middle schoolers sometimes make up stories in order to impress others?

DEPRESSED AND FEELING ALONE

As the principal sat there listening to the young man share how depressed he was, she wondered how he had gotten to this state and why a young man that seemed to have so much going for him felt so desolate. In front of his friends he was the class clown and full of life. No one would know he was hurting so much on the inside until he finally shared it with a friend, a guidance counselor, or a teacher.

This young man had tried to cut himself, and he wanted to run as far away as possible and not come back, but he had nowhere to go. Several times every year it seemed that Mrs. James would be working with a student that was calling out for help. Often the student would share that he or she didn't care about living anymore. Grades were no longer important, nor was the idea of passing or failing. A suicide contract would be drawn up and the parents would be notified with a witness present. Each incident like this one received immediate attention and was treated very seriously.

Teens talk about struggles in their homes where they feel like they are being treated unfairly and the lack of being able to talk to their parents, are concerned when their parents struggle with anxiety and depression, and are affected by divorce when their parents decide it's the thing to do. Teens with depression also express that they feel like something is "wrong" with them. They want to be normal and they want to be heard.

WHY THEY DO WHAT THEY DO

From an emotional standpoint, adolescence represents something akin to Murphy's Law: anything that can go wrong will go wrong. At a national conference on adolescence, the keynote speaker reminded his audience that adolescence is not a single process, but a suite of changes that occur at different times and with different intensities.[14]

For a long time, it was generally believed that a teenager's mood swings and emotional reactivity were due solely to raging hormones produced and released during puberty. This is partly true. But while fluctuations in hormone levels are a major contributor to teenagers' mood swings, there is much more to adolescent emotions than hormones.

Oh, there are hormones involved all right. The biggies, of course, are the gonadal hormones that stimulate the release of estrogen and testosterone. But these sex hormones represent only a portion of the many brain chemicals that can affect an adolescent's post-pubertal emotional status. Some chemicals exert a direct effect on emotions, while others exert their effects indirectly.

For example, growth hormones are responsible for the rapid physical development that occurs during adolescence. Depending on how it goes, growing a new body and then adjusting to it can pose a significant emotional challenge for some teens. An obvious example includes girls who reach puberty early, say, in late elementary school. When they return for the start of middle school they are conspicuous in size and shape and they are a curiosity (as well as an object of teasing) to classmates. Talk about a difficult emotional challenge!

Boys can suffer a similar emotional fate, not because they reach puberty before everyone else, but because they reach it later than everyone else. Boys with late-onset puberty can only watch with envy as one boy after another becomes taller, more muscular, and more mature. And there is nothing they can do but wait until the puberty fairy finally visits them. What a helpless feeling this must be, especially for boys trying to define who they are.

Generally speaking, the onset of puberty occurs earlier and is somewhat more difficult for girls than it is for boys. For boys, reaching puberty provides bragging rights and superior physical skills as testosterone replaces baby fat with muscle. For girls, puberty means learning to manage one more obligation and to adjust to physical changes that often attract the kind of comments and attention that most girls are not seeking. Once the long-anticipated event finally does arrive, many girls experience some mild confusion and anxiety. Now what?

Their bodies start changing in ways they hadn't planned, their complexion fails them, even their hair changes. Most of all they have a new body (and new feelings about this body) and they don't know what to do with either. Adjusting to a new body, especially one that wasn't requested, can be emotionally difficult for both boys and girls. Adjusting comes at a price, and much of the cost comes in the form of confusion and conflicting emotions.

Some hormones and some neurotransmitters affect emotions more directly. Throughout this book there is a recurring theme that structural and chemical changes strengthen some skills and weaken others. This holds true for emotions as well. Whereas some brain changes make it possible for teens to feel new and more intense emotions, other changes make them feel anxious, sad, and stressed.

Research conducted by Deborah Yurgelun-Todd at Harvard's McLean Hospital reveals that young teens (middle schoolers) do poorly on tasks that require them to identify emotions based on a person's facial expression. It was found that young teens tend to activate the amygdala (a brain structure than senses fear) whereas adults activate the brain's frontal lobes (the region we use for careful deliberation).[15]

Less able to access the frontal lobes, the young teenage brain recruits what it can; in this case, the amygdala. The problem in activating this region is that it causes the brain to overreact, because it perceives threats that may not be there.

The immaturity of the frontal lobes also explains why teenagers, especially young teens, have difficulty with affect regulation. Affect regulation is the ability to modulate or control one's emotions and to inhibit one's responses to incoming sensory information. During the adolescent years, teens gradually develop the ability to regulate affect so that emotions support rather than interfere with decision making.[16]

Some debate this assertion, arguing that teens possess the ability to think calmly and rationally. True enough. In fact, these are called cool cognitions. The problem is that teens frequently try to make decisions when they are highly aroused and feeling strong emotions. These are called hot cognitions; they're the ones that lead to reckless and dangerous decisions. Once the frontal lobes mature sufficiently, teens are able to moderate amygdala responses and to dampen the emotional reactivity it generates.

And what of those sudden bursts of passion or affection teens suddenly feel for some peers? Another critical change occurring during adolescence is the development and refinement of connections between the brain's cognitive and affective centers. It is crucial that these regions connect, because rational decision making is based, in part, on whether we believe that a certain decision will make us happy, sad, or apprehensive.

But in young teens, these systems have not yet matured fully and romantic passion can easily overwhelm rational thinking. The story of *Romeo and Juliet* is the classic example of passion overwhelming one's ability to reason, to consider consequences, to wait for cool cognitions, and to inhibit one's actions. And it is worth noting that in Shakespeare's play for the ages, Juliet is thirteen years old, a middle schooler.

It has been well established that depression, anxiety, and stress increase during adolescence. For some, this is the beginning of a life-long struggle with mood disorders. For most teens, however, these are transient changes that diminish as the prefrontal cortex matures and modulates the amygdala's hyperreactivity.

But during early adolescence, the amygdala plays a dominant role in interpreting social cues. The problem with the amygdala is that its main function is to recognize threats and to trigger the fight-or-flight response. It's supposed to do that. It's just that the amygdala matures before the prefrontal cortex, and instead of relying on the prefrontal cortex to interpret the social cues and the emotions of others, early adolescents tend to rely on the amygdala.

Thus, when parents and teachers assume an angry or threatening posture, the teenager's brain sends this information to the amygdala to interpret (or misinterpret) the adult's facial expression. And because of its role in fight or flight, the amygdala response leads to increased arousal and heightened emotions. This is good for survival, but not so good when negotiating curfews and discussing report cards.

In addition to emotional hyperarousal, the misinterpretation of other's emotional cues also leads to increased anxiety and stress in teenagers. To make matters even worse, anxious teenagers ruminate about (and sometimes obsess over) their anxious feelings, a process that can send some of them into despair and, without some relief, depression. The stress response is even more direct. Once the amygdala warns the adrenal glands that a threat is present, the adrenal glands secrete cortisol, the stress hormone that triggers the fight-or-flight response.

And then mother nature plays one of her cruel and inexplicable tricks. In addition to cortisol, there is another hormone released when the brain responds to stress. In adults, this hormone reduces anxiety. But in teens, it has the opposite effect, because the receptor sites that respond to it actually increase just after puberty. Eventually, these extra receptors will die off, but in the intervening years, the increased availability of receptor sites actually cause an increase in anxiety. Wouldn't you know.

And then there are the sex hormones. With the onset of puberty, the hypothalamus produces gonadotropin releasing hormone (GnRH) and sends it into the pituitary gland. From there, the GnRH travels to the sex organs where it causes the release of estrogen and progesterone in girls and testosterone in boys. Once released, these sex hormones create a host of physical changes in male and female bodies.

Though these changes are meant to serve a simple biological function (reproduction of the species), the changes create emotional havoc in the person whose body suddenly starts to change. Too bad for you—mother nature considers reproduction more important than self-image. Get over it.

Although these body changes are more than sufficiently challenging, the sex hormones are not finished just yet. One of the more insidious effects of both estrogen and testosterone is that they induce the skin's oil glands to produce more oil than usual. When these excess oils mix with dirt and dead skin cells, the combination can block the pores in the skin. The blockage can be in the form of a blackhead, a whitehead, or a cyst—in other words, acne.

And oil glands aren't the only glands affected by pubertal hormones. Sweat glands also become more active, producing not just more moisture, but more odors as well.

There is one more hormonal culprit that contributes to the anxiety, stress, and the general emotional turmoil of adolescence. This is the hormone oxytocin. Sometimes dubbed the love hormone, oxytocin release is related to feelings of attachment. The increased level of this hormone explains why teenagers seem to be constantly seeking the company of close friends, why they begin to pair off in couples, and why they so easily fall in love. The other time that oxytocin increases is just after childbirth, which helps to explain mother-infant bonding.

Emotional upheaval is a hallmark of adolescence. Nowhere is the relationship between puberty and adolescence more evident than in teenagers' emotional ups and downs, because it is here that the introduction of new hormones exerts its influence. In previous chapters we learned that the adolescent brain is not so good at inhibition. In this chapter we learned that hormones and other neurochemicals are providing the energy that the teenage brain seems incapable of inhibiting.

Although the major culprits are the sex hormones (testosterone and estrogen), we now know that the chemical picture is far more complex. It is good to be reminded that Juliet was only thirteen, because this helps us to appreciate the level of depression, anxiety, and stress that young adolescents experience. It is a time when everything in the brain seems to be working against teens. Eventually brain structures and brain chemicals will come into balance, but it is essential for adults to remember that during these difficult years, teenagers really do struggle with circumstances far beyond their control.

Chapter 13

Powerful Points from Middle Schoolers

A group of middle schoolers, ages eleven to fourteen, was asked if given the opportunity, what they would say to their teachers that would make their school experience better and what they would tell their parents that would make their home life better. The students were told that their responses would be anonymous and that their parents had given them written permission to participate in this activity.

With great sincerity and dedication they went to work, some for up to two hours, diligently writing down what they would tell their parents and teachers. They felt like this was their chance to be heard without any repercussions. Although spelling mistakes have been corrected in this chapter, the words belong completely to eleven- to fourteen-year-old students.

TEENS TALKING TO TEACHERS

A thirteen-year-old boy:

> Good teachers equal good learning. It's a simple concept, in theory. But what makes a good teacher? I think they have to care, and by that I mean they have to care about their students, care about what they're learning and care about the quality of the content being delivered. I think a teacher needs to want to do more than just follow a lesson plan, assign different worksheets and hold standard, end of period exams.
>
> Teachers should encourage their students to do well, whether it be a gold star or a point of extra credit or even a party if grades improve. Even a simple "Nice Job!" or "Good Work!" lightens up a student's day and improves the quality of work they put forth. If a child hears a "Nice Work!" they'll want to do even

better to get another "Great Job!" because that sort of thing really brightens your day.

Now of course, if a child isn't doing well, a more correct course of action wouldn't be to scold the child, but to help. Really, if you scold a child for doing poorly, you're making matters worse. It lowers their self-esteem and in doing so lowers their work ethics, overall thoughts about school. It's a reverse of encouragement—it makes kids feel awful about themselves and their work. In a few cases, this enabled kids to want to do better, but usually this doesn't come without help.

However, I realize there may be extenuating circumstances, for instance, if a teacher is having a bad day or suffering the loss of a loved one, it can be incredibly hard to do your job as a teacher. That's why I regard teaching as one of the hardest professions in our workforce. You're in charge of approximately 180 kids over the course of eight class periods, 180 working days of the year.

And, you have to keep track of their grades, behavior, attendance . . . with so many things to keep up with, it's impossible for me to blame teachers in any sort of way. But, if they encouraged and helped kids, it would make their jobs easier overall. They wouldn't have to watch grades or behaviors nearly as much as before.

Overall, I think teachers should be fair, encouraging, helpful, and, in the simplest sense, they have to care. I know teachers have an extremely hard job. But if they just encouraged good behavior, helped students who are doing poorly, and cared, truly cared, about the quality of our education, it would make their job—and our job—a lot easier.

A fourteen-year-old girl:

In the classrooms I think that students should be treated with respect. They [teachers] should teach us no different from any other child in this school. We come to school obviously to learn new things in life. I think the teacher should be sincere with us and understand some problems that we might have, or need to share to them. They should be open to tell them anything. Some teachers can be a little on the harsh side sometimes. But others you can tell anything that you need. And you can trust them with your thoughts and understandings towards situations.

What are these youngsters asking for? Simply for teachers to care about them and to treat them with respect. The boy is even willing to understand if teachers have a bad day or are grieving the loss of a loved one; the girl is simply asking the same in return. The boy acknowledges that teachers have a lot to keep track of and a lot of students to care for. But if teachers would encourage and help, their jobs would be easier. The girl is seeking trust. Both students are seeking relationships.

In an earlier chapter we learned that relationships mitigate the dangerous parts of adolescence. Strangely, teenagers know what they need. They don't always go about it in the way that adults want them to, but they know.

A twelve-year-old boy:

I would tell them that they should involve something fun instead of "Here you go, get started." Some teachers are fun and some are really strict. I think they should be both. Some of the really strict teachers don't have room for mistakes. Some are fun, but have lots of room for mistakes resulting in bullying and in foolishness in our classrooms. I like a quiet environment when I am working on a really important assignment, but when there are fun assignments I like to talk to people while we work.

A fourteen-year-old girl:

To me, a great teacher is one that is always enthusiastic and is happy to be around her students. They should always encourage questions and never roll their eyes at us. I hate it when a teacher always has a scowl on her face, it makes me feel afraid to ask or answer questions because it seems like she will go off on me. My favorite teachers find creative ways to make the class more entertaining.

Some teachers don't get that we don't want to sit there and read out of a boring textbook every day. We also don't appreciate having to do dull worksheets that we get nothing out of. I would much rather prefer the teacher to show us examples on the board and call on students to answer the questions. I find that being interactive with the class and the teacher really helps me learn better.

Good teachers take it further than just the time given to them to teach. They go out of their way to help their students. For example, my math teacher lets us stay after school to finish a test or if we need help on a certain subject. She always helps one on one, this makes me feel that she wants us to learn and succeed. She jokes around with us keeping us attentive and the class fun. These are all characteristics I believe a good teacher should have.

A thirteen-year-old girl:

A teacher should treat people with respect and kindness. She shouldn't be harsh whenever you ask questions. The kind of teacher I would be able to talk to whenever something is bothering me is one who understands you and does the best they can to help you out. A great class environment I would say is one where you cannot only get a group lesson, but if you were having trouble with a specific part they can give you more one-on-one time to make sure you can do it.

A teacher should act like they actually care about you and your grades and help you set and achieve a goal throughout the year. They should be more caring about your feelings and their attitude must be positive. A teacher that makes me feel like I can't ask questions is when you ask maybe "Could you explain my grade and why I have it?" and they wouldn't laugh in your face about it.

A fourteen-year-old boy:

For me, a great classroom environment is a brightly lit room with lots of colorful posters, books, and clean desks and chairs. Bright lights (but no blinding lights) help me stay awake and alert. Colorful posters are fun and great to learn with. Clean desks and chairs make me want to study. Also, an added benefit would be a few comfy chairs for reading days. It is nice to be in a class with students who are ready to participate and learn, but also have fun. Also, it is nice to learn from a variety of sources (not just a textbook) such as reference books, the internet, and videos.

A teacher that I would like to talk to would be one that is kind and patient, yet has control over a class. A teacher that would be hard to talk to would be one that is angry a lot and one that has favorites and would only listen to those few people. I know that it can be hard not to have favorites. I volunteered to help little 3-year-olds at my dance studio as they started dancing and some of them were so much more cooperative and friendly than others. However, I try to be fair with each of them and play with all of them.

A twelve-year-old girl:

I could tell teachers how I would like to be treated and what makes me learn the most each day. I would say that I like to be talked to kindly and that lecturing doesn't help me learn at all. An environment with motivational posters and bright colors makes me feel good and helps me learn. Teachers that are kind and fair are easy to talk to but some teachers get mad when you ask them to repeat something or explain something. This makes me feel like I can't ask them questions that help me learn.

A fourteen-year-old girl:

What makes a good teacher for me would be if they acted friendly towards the students and taught with a laid back sort of way. I feel that if the teacher actually shows that he or she cares about the ideas and opinions that I have, then I would feel more compelled to pay attention in class, and actually care about learning the lesson. In past experiences I found that the more uptight or stressed the teacher is, the less respect they get from the students around me.

Most kids, including me, don't respond well towards fast-paced or demanding teachers/ways of learning. When the teacher is negative towards us, we get upset and eventually stop paying attention because we think that if the teacher doesn't care enough to put a smile on her face, then why should we?

A thirteen-year-old girl:

One of my best teachers is the kind of person I would choose as a best friend. They are understanding, fun, and most importantly, a good teacher. They are not boring and they do not hesitate to aid you in any way possible. I feel and know, that no matter what I ask, or do, or say, they will always be honest, and will always be there.

On the rare occasion in which I am uncomfortable with a teacher, I become very quiet and keep to myself (quite opposite than my usual personality). When it gets to the point when I don't feel as if I can ask a question, it's bad. To me, the atmosphere is tense and pressured. I feel as if the teacher is rushing, and I would be disturbing the learning process by asking anything.

Honestly, I rarely have teachers I dislike or am not comfortable with, but even when I do, I get through it. I know that all teachers have our best interests at heart, and as long as you keep that in mind, it's always okay. I cannot begin to thank all my teachers for everything they do for me, but I hope they know I'm grateful.

A fourteen-year-old boy:

I don't need to ask questions about what we are learning, but every once in a while I do, and sometimes the teacher doesn't seem willing to answer the questions. Those teachers tend to talk quickly, and tend to be more prone to give students disciplinary marks. For most students they seem to feel like if they ask a question, they will be yelled at. In the classes that they teach, most of the time the students have to learn on their own, and it is much harder for the student [to] comprehend and learn that skill or lesson. However, more of my teachers are easy to talk to, and I don't suffer for the ones who aren't.

One of my favorite teachers is my Geometry teacher. One of the reasons she is my favorite, is because I have known her all three years . . . The other reason she is a good teacher, is when she is teaching you feel like you can ask her questions, and she won't think you are stupid for them. She listens to you and if you make a good point she will compliment you for it.

She is not quick to assume you are doing something that will earn you a mark. She gives you plenty of time to work on class work and homework. The pace of her class is quick, but she gives us ample time to work out some things if you don't get it. A teacher who is nice, familiar, but also very good at teaching her subject is probably my idea of a perfect teacher.

Isn't it interesting? We tend to think of adolescents as surly, oppositional, defiant, and too independent. But here are typical adolescents and what are they asking for? They want to have a close relationship with their teachers. Who would have thought? And they don't want teachers to think they are stupid. They know they don't think well and that they are sometimes dense.

You can almost hear them say, "But please don't remind us. And most of all don't remind us when other kids are around."

It is also clear that they are just trying to get their needs met. They want an education and they want their teachers to help them. And they want to succeed. They also want to have fun, but is that so abnormal? Getting ready for school, getting to school, being in school, getting home from school, and doing homework account for more than ten hours of a student's day. Does anyone want to spend most of their waking hours in misery?

When kids ask that learning be fun, they are not asking for entertainment. Rather, they are asking that it be safe, enjoyable, and rewarding. When you consider that about one-third of our brain is made up of reward circuits, their request does not seem so strange after all.

TEENS TALKING TO PARENTS

A twelve-year-old boy:

> If I could I would say you need to make more time where we can do things to-gether. The life at my house would be a lot easier if it was a little more relaxed and not so on the "GoGoGo!" No, I don't feel like I can talk with my parent about everything because I'm afraid that they will get mad at me. If they would not yell as much there would be a quiet conversation about the subject. I am careful of what I talk about because they might blow up on me and that would probably be bad for our relationship.

A fourteen-year-old girl:

> One thing that would make my life easier as a middle school student would be the ability to talk to my parents about things that are going on, without getting ridiculed for it. Say I got an F on a test, I know it's a terrible grade, and I know that I could have done better if I studied harder. So instead of giving me a hour long lecture about that things I already know, try being considerate and instead of getting all hot-headed about it, stay calm and offer to help me study for the next test, or try to help me find out what I did wrong when managing my time studying.
>
> If my parents did that for me I'd be making 100 percent on every test I take. Another thing that would make home life easier would be actually giving me a reserved amount of time where everything would be quiet and peaceful so I can really focus on my homework assignments and do the best work I can possibly do. I love my parents but, if something were bothering me they wouldn't neces-sarily be the first ones I would go to for advice.

In my eyes, my parents are just that—parental figures, and I just don't feel 100 percent comfortable discussing social matters with them.

I would turn to a friend my age for help over my parents any day because my parents have a tendency to hold things over my head for long periods of time, or at least until the next embarrassing thing happens, and they switch to that one. I would feel more comfortable discussing these things with them if they would show a little empathy towards me, and try to find some way to help me with the problem at hand. I'm careful about what I talk about around them because if I accidentally tell them too much about a personal matter, they might go around spreading it to their friends, or never let me forget it.

A twelve-year-old boy:

I would tell my parents that when I need help with something not to make me go step-by-step and figure it out myself. I would want them to walk me through it and help me with the problem. I would think that if I needed to talk to my parents I would want them to be understanding and come from my point of view. And when I come to them with a problem I would hope that they won't yell at me and get all mad.

In each case, these youngsters are asking that they not be ridiculed, criticized, made to feel incompetent. Here we have a twelve-year-old boy who is already aware that he must self-censor so that he does not make his parents mad. At twelve, he is protecting the relationship! And parents think they have no influence over their teenagers!

A fourteen-year-old girl:

My parents are getting divorced and I feel like I don't really get along with my dad so I go to my mom with everything. I talk to her about boys, school, soccer, how I feel, anything! With my dad it's totally different because I don't really get along with him because we always butt heads when he like asks me all these questions. I just wish they understood what I feel and how I feel about them getting a divorce, sometimes I wish I could freeze time and fix everything.

A fourteen-year-old girl:

My life would be so much easier if my mom wasn't so judging. I wish she'd be more calm and accepted me as I am. If only she understood that I am not perfect, that I can't do everything right at my first attempt, I would be happier. One day I hope she realizes that I don't want to live her dreams. I want to accomplish mine. I have my own goals, aspirations, and hopes. She has no right to control me. One day she may tell me that I can talk to her about anything and the next she'll throw a fit because I told the truth. These are only a few things that she could change; there are many other things other kids are wishing their parents would change.

I think that if parents were more understanding and less dramatic, kids would be less rebellious. If they put more effort toward trying to comprehend us, we would tell them more things. We want to live our own lives; we want to experience the world through our own eyes, not our parents' experiences. All these things make our lives miserable, being accepted for who we are by our parents is what all of kids seek.

An eleven-year-old girl:

It makes me feel better when I talk to them. When I tell them about something, my mom and dad discuss it, then act right away, but usually they ask me my opinion. That's what I like about them. I could talk about almost anything with them. Only sometimes will they not get it and I have to speak more carefully. I still like them, because they always help me be a better student.

A twelve-year-old girl:

I would want to say to them things that would make them understand that I can be very adult-like and I want to be treated the way I would want to be treated—like an adult. Sometimes being a middle school kid would make you want to change, like wearing makeup or going to the movies with your friends alone.

Your parents might say no but if you can show that you are responsible enough to show what you can do to be treated the way you want. Just like if you wanted a puppy, you have to show your parents responsibility. So, all I have to say is that being in middle school can make you change and parents have to do the same.

A fourteen-year-old boy:

One of the biggest reasons I succeed in school is because of my parents. When my parents check the grades online it is one of the most helpful things they could do. Every day asking me if I have any tests, homework, or projects due keeps my grades in line. I can't imagine how my grades would be without my parents checking up on me. It turns into such a pain and becomes very annoying but seeing how much it helps me at the end of the grading period I am very grateful.

Life at my house is really good. I have good parents and good friends and I think that reflects greatly on my school work. I feel that I can talk about anything with my parents because they always remind me of it. But sometimes I am careful about what I say because I feel that my parents just don't need to know everything about my life. That would really be weird to me.

A twelve-year-old girl:

I would tell all the drama that's at school in sixth grade because I'm always in it. We could talk about it at home because talking to my dad always makes me feel better. Yes, I would be able to talk about it with my parents. They always comfort me and make me feel safe, and sometimes they call the principal and talk about it.

I am careful of what I talk about because I am not allowed to date or have boyfriends yet, and because I come to school to learn, not be in drama. Plus about drama, it develops this whole fake you and it's made up. So if someone was describing you to someone else, it's a whole bunch of lies, it wouldn't even actually even sound like you. Don't judge a book by its cover.

A fourteen-year-old girl:

Sometimes your parents can be a little bit unsympathetic to what a middle schooler is going through. Your parents forget what it feels like to start changing mentally and physically while trying to fit the image as the perfect person for your peers. My parents are great, but sometimes it feels like they over work me. I am sent for everything. I don't really mind all that much but sometimes it gets in the way of things I need to do, like homework or reading.

My sister is really sweet most of the time, but sometimes she can be a bit of a pain. It is hard to explain, but the older sister in me always wants to be better and sometimes I'm not. Whatever they do though, I always love my family dearly.

A twelve-year-old girl:

I would like if my parents would stop comparing me to other students and worrying about my grades. I feel like telling them "I'm in seventh grade! I can handle my own grades." But if I tell them that, I'll get in trouble for being disrespectful. I am careful about what I say to my parents because if I say something they don't like, they'll ask too many questions and find something with whatever I did and I'll get in trouble.

Also, my parents say that because of me, my sister is behaving bad and that I'm the root of the problem when half the time, I'm NOT! It's completely unfair. My parents give me NO freedom. I can't text. They check all my e-mails, and they monitor my phone calls. I feel like I need more freedom.

A fourteen-year-old boy:

If I could tell my parents something to make my middle school life easier, I would tell them to stop telling me what homework I need to do and stop comparing me to other kids above my level. Life could be easier at home because I would have more time to do other things even after finishing my school work. I want to talk about everything to my parents, but I can't all the time. Whenever I try to talk about things that we never really talk about I want them to be open and listen to everything I say.

I really don't want them to criticize me on what I say, which they do a lot. I go to my mom the most because she is calm and she understands better than my dad. I'm careful about what I talk to my parents (about) because I don't want them to feel as if I can't be mature and handle things myself.

A fourteen-year-old girl:

I think it would be easier to have a little more supportive parents. Life would be easier if my parents understood that I can balance working hard and getting to be with friends. They believe that a lot of things (such as Facebook) are distractions. I definitely understand where they are coming from. But if they just gave me a chance, maybe I could balance and not get distracted. I think that I can talk about anything with my parents. They always stress that I can talk about anything with them and are really trying to do what's best for me.

A thirteen-year-old girl:

Something I would tell parents is "Stop comparing . . . to his/her older sibling, they are NOT in the same grade and obviously have a different learning process." No one is ever the same related or not so parents shouldn't compare young kids to older kids. It makes the student feel as if they are not living up to your expectations and makes them feel bad about themselves.

My parents' act about school is very calm. Whenever my grades are low they encourage me and tell me to do my best. They don't take away events or objects. But for some people it makes work. If students are purposely failing in a class, yes that is definitely a reason to take away an object (phone, computer, etc.) but even when the student is doing their best, to their parent their best isn't enough so there goes a phone when it wasn't the student's fault. Making that student feel not good enough and maybe even drop out of school.

A thirteen-year-old girl:

As teenagers, it feels as if we are in a never-ending war against our parents. Some parents try to be cool and some just are themselves. But no matter how they act, no teenager has ever been embarrassed by them. But, no matter how much we complain, at the end of the day, you love them. And that's all there is to it.

My parents are very open and very understanding, and that definitely prevents stress (because I already have enough of that). But, even though I know that I can talk about anything with them and that they will be honest and loving all the same, I admit I hesitate. Some things just aren't easy to talk about. And it kills me that I don't have the guts to confront them about things but, it's just hard.

I am so grateful for everything my parents have done and do for me that it's difficult and daunting to ask anything more from them. But, to be honest a little more space and freedom would be nice. Sometimes they are like helicopters hovering over me and I feel as if there is little to no wiggle room (although with all of the other things in my life stressing me I'm sure that they get emphasized a little more than they are in actuality). But then again at other points, it seems as if they are disconnected from me completely. Like our long-distance phone call was ended suddenly. But to my relief, it eventually reconnects.

I'm sure that the stress of middle school and social lives adds to the effect of our parents, but I wouldn't give them up for anything in the world. I may not ever win the war against them, but I will gladly accept my loss (although this is the only circumstance in which I will accept failure) and will, of course, love them forever.

A thirteen-year-old boy:

I personally think what a parent should do is very much what a teacher should do: help, encourage and care. However, of the three, caring matters the most. Something as simple as asking "How was your day?" shows you care. Parents should also care about what their child thinks or wants to know. Children should be able to go up to their parents and ask anything, whether it is a math problem or asking how they (the child) came into this world.

No topics should be restricted, because a child should be able to have a conversation with his/her parents and ask or talk or confess about any topic. Kids shouldn't have to rely on the internet or their friends for unreliable or confusing information. Parents should encourage discussions between them and their child. They should make it feel normal to talk about otherwise embarrassing or heartbreaking things.

A child should never feel discouraged about talking to their parents. They should feel relaxed and calm about talking (about) even the most embarrassing things. They should be able to talk about school, talk about boy/girl friends, and talk about how school is going as well as their concerns (tests, bullying, etc.) with their parents.

The biggest thing is that it shouldn't be restricted. It should be encouraged and welcomed. Being able to learn and connect with their parents will strengthen their bond and help the child better understand the life they are taking on. Without this source of knowledge they would go into life unprepared and unready for life's challenges.

Parents: Would you want your child to be unready for the future?

A twelve-year-old boy:

Parents are also a big help with making us students learn in middle school. Sometimes they help you with homework, sometimes they get on to you for getting a bad grade or doing something wrong, for math homework, and they congratulate us on our report card for getting good grades. But it doesn't matter because you might not know it but they're always looking out for you and doing whatever it takes to make us happy. The best thing is that you can talk to them about anything you want . . .

So yah, parents are a big part of middle school in many ways. NO matter how "bumbly" things get they're always there for you. No matter what the course is, they're parents and they love you. That's how they affect you and middle school.

WHY THEY DO WHAT THEY DO

William Glasser is a well-known psychiatrist who has developed a model for creating quality schools. One of the key features of quality schools is that they rid themselves of what he calls the seven deadly habits. These seven include blaming, complaining, nagging, threatening, criticizing, punishing, and rewarding. Neither students nor teachers can use any of the seven deadly habits, because they interfere with the two primary goals of education: doing quality work and building relationships.

Once rid of the seven deadly habits, teachers and administrators replace them with the seven connecting habits. These include caring, listening, supporting, contributing, encouraging, trusting, and befriending. These are connecting habits, because they accomplish a critical feature of quality schools: that teachers build supportive relationships with their students. The student writings that appear above are a testament to Glasser's experience and wisdom. Whether they are writing to their parents or to their teachers, the students are asking them to do precisely what Glasser recommends.

One of the recurring themes in these writings is how readily students acknowledge the positive impact their parents and teachers have on their lives. Without prompting, they freely admit that they benefit from the love and support their parents provide. We really do matter to them, despite how it feels when they are embarrassed to be seen with us in public. At the same time, though, they plead with parents and teachers to be more understanding and more accepting.

In the teacher section, they want their teachers to care about them. They will care in return. But caring is an important theme. And they don't mind working hard, if it is legitimate work. They know busy work when they see it, and they hate busy work. But they never complain about their school work being too hard. They want their teachers to be good, but they want them to be understanding and to provide them with help willingly when needed. And please, they ask, don't make us feel stupid. When you think of it, they really aren't asking for very much, are they?

And it's the same with parents. Stop yelling, stop criticizing, and stop comparing me to others. Most of all, they want their parents to talk to them. They don't want any topics to be off limits and they don't want their parents to get mad about what they choose to disclose. Their peers don't, so they talk to peers. But they want to talk to parents too. They also want to be understood. They want parents and teachers to appreciate that adolescence is a difficult journey and that don't get everything right every time.

What is so evident in these writings is the adolescent dilemma. On the one hand, we have a teenager who is seeking to be understood, to be trusted, to be given more responsibility, and to be treated with respect. On the other hand, there are parents and teachers who don't trust the child to make the right decisions and to consider the consequences before making a decision.

To be sure, the adolescent brain is not yet ready for adult problem solving and it is not very good at controlling impulses. But we also know that with the onset of puberty, forces are set in motion that impel our children to seek more control over their lives and to want to take on more responsibility.

These brain changes make adolescence a difficult time for parents, teachers, and for teens. But one of the things that comes through in these student musings is that it is not the titanic battles over drugs, sex, and school that are the problem. Rather, in school and at home, it is the unkind comment, the lack of trust, and the fear of expressing their opinions that are on the minds of most teens.

Their brains are telling them to do one thing, their parents are telling them to do the opposite. Their brains are telling them to go faster, their parents are insisting that they slow down. Their parents are telling them it is time to go to sleep, their brains are telling them stay up for another hour or two.

One of the fourteen-year-old girls wrote, "I don't want to live her dreams. I want to accomplish mine." Notice that she uses the word accomplish. She is not requesting that anything be given to her; she is quite willing to accomplish her goals. She wants to experience that sense of accomplishment that we can only get when doing it ourselves.

She also reminds all of us that rebellion is in some way a reaction to her parents' behavior toward her. It would be difficult to find a better way to explain that adolescence is a time when our children begin to develop their own identity, that teens want to be adult-like, that they don't always get it right. But they also want the support and the understanding of their parents and teachers during this struggle.

The recurring theme to parents and teachers is that teenagers freely acknowledge (at least in the privacy of these letters) that they don't have it all figured out yet. They admit their shortcomings and their fears and then they ask for our understanding and our assistance. What a wonderful thing to know about this much-maligned group!

They couldn't be any more clear. Stop yelling, stop criticizing, and stop comparing me to others. Most parents and teachers are not going to have to fight the titanic battles over drugs, sexual promiscuity, or academic failure. What concerns most teens is that we care about them and that we respect them. Though they want to do it on their terms, they really do want to talk to adults. But they are seeking a two-way conversation, they are begging to be heard.

Chapter 14

Reflections

After Mrs. Bolton, the principal, asked "So . . . who put the booger on your binder?" she stood there in thoughtful silence waiting for thirteen-year-old Jessica's answer. She couldn't believe that her job involved asking such an unusual question to another human being. But this human being, as we know, is one of many human beings of middle school age "out there." Jessica, a pretty blonde with lots of energy, had squealed out a noise when everyone else was quietly leaving the cafeteria after lunch.

As principal, Mrs. Bolton had asked her to remain in the cafeteria to explain why she was the only person she heard making such a loud noise. Jessica shared with Mrs. Bolton that someone had put a booger on her binder. She had wiped it off and then he had put it back on. Mrs. Bolton didn't hear the name and asked "So . . . who put the booger on your binder?" Why did HER job entail such a question at her place of employment?

Middle school students are learning and growing, but contrary to popular belief, they are great to be around. This young lady had screamed out in the lunchroom during dismissal time. In the principal's "wisdom," she needed to know why Jessica had squealed while everyone else was leaving the lunchroom in a reasonable fashion. But this is middle school life . . . asking questions like this, learning to laugh and sometimes cry right along with our middle school charges.

How best to deal with middle schoolers at home and in school leaves many unanswered questions. In 2008, Newt Gingrich wrote an article in *Business Week* in which he called for the complete abolition of adolescence. Calling it a failed experiment of the nineteenth century, he argues that throughout history and even in some modern cultures, one is a child until the onset of puberty, at which time one becomes an adult.

He cites examples from history, including Benjamin Franklin, who was apprenticed to his brother at age thirteen and Daniel Boone, who was an expert hunter and explorer by age fourteen. He also notes that students typically entered college at the age of thirteen or fourteen.[17]

Gingrich makes some valid points. Our current educational system does move too slowly for some children. There are few options available for highly motivated students who are ready to begin college prior to high school graduation, as well as for students who have no intention of going to college and wish to begin working full time prior to high school graduation. Prolonging adolescence inhibits their growth and prevents them from accepting adult responsibilities they are fully prepared to accept.

In a way, Gingrich's challenge to end adolescence is a classic case of which came first: Is adolescence a social construct, invented to serve some social or economic purpose? Or have cultural norms and expectations changed to accommodate a real and unique stage of human development?

The simple answer is that probably both are true. Many teens are ready for more responsibility than they are given. In the Amish community, for example, some boys as young as fourteen or fifteen are well on their way to becoming master carpenters. But lest we forget, the Amish also have that wonderful custom of *rumspringa* when teenagers are given the opportunity to hang out with peers and to experiment with life outside the community.

Two hundred years ago, it may have been common for some individuals to assume adult responsibilities. Alexander the Great was conquering much of the known world when he was nineteen. But the most famous people in history may have been blessed with extraordinary talents. It would be interesting to know what their less-endowed peers were up to at age thirteen.

When it comes to understanding adolescence and adolescents, we are at an interesting intersection. On the one hand, modern American culture probably delays adulthood for most teens. At the same time, however, neuroscientists are beginning to find explanations of why teens since the time of Socrates make decisions that don't make sense, take life-threatening risks, experience mood swings, and drive parents and teachers to the breaking point. So while the idea of a teenager may have started as an advertiser's creation, there is ample evidence from across time and across cultures that something important is happening between ages twelve and twenty.

Franklin, Boone, and Alexander the Great notwithstanding, it is our responsibility to address the adolescent situation as it exists in modern America culture, circa 2011. Part of this obligation is to shed as much light as we can on the largely unexplained and mysterious process of adolescent development. This light comes from various sources: human development, social psychology, anthropology, and, more recently, genetics and the neurosciences.

First and foremost, adolescence is a time of identity formation. In primitive cultures, in feudal societies, and in agrarian societies, identity is defined almost exclusively by one's social status or by the occupation of a family member. Until very recently chances were good that if your father was a farmer, you were going to a farmer. Cultural systems in which one's occupation and social status are predetermined greatly simplify identity formation. But American youth, especially those born after World War II, enjoy a broad range of vocational, religious, social, and marriage options.

With so many choices available, identity formation is far more complicated for the typical American teenager than it was for most of history and for most teens (especially girls) in developing nations or in nations with little or no social mobility. Although higher family income and parent education provide distinct advantages for some, it might be argued that most American youth have too many choices. Sorting through these choices takes time as teenagers discover and then experiment with various *selves* until they discover one that suits them.

To say that we can or should do away with adolescence is to suggest that a person at age thirteen is able to select an occupation, choose a faith (or not), determine an appropriate educational plan, select a political party, begin a family, and make all the other decisions that adults make. The problem is not that modern American culture has intentionally prolonged childhood. Rather, the dilemma facing American children is that they have so many choices that it may just take longer to consider which ones fit and which don't.

As if identity formation alone were not enough of a challenge, it happens to coincide with a time when the brain is going through significant changes. The brain of a typical five- or six-year-old child has achieved about 95 percent of its adult size. Until recently, it was assumed that except for some minor modifications, the brain of a child functioned more or less like the brain of an adult. In the past two decades, however, advances in neuroimaging have revealed that the brain remodels and reshapes itself well into early adulthood.

Puberty has always been seen as the crucial event signaling the transition from childhood to adulthood. For a long time, the focus of puberty was confined mainly to one's reproductive capacity and the sex hormones that came with it. Recently, however, new research is revealing that virtually all developmental abilities are influenced to a greater or lesser extent with the onset of puberty. The changes that occur are not confined to the production of sex hormones.

For example, there is a rapid thickening in the gray matter of the brain that occurs as neurons make many more connections with each other. These new connections are essential. They provide the capacity to manage the more

complex demands of adulthood. Taking care of a newborn is more complicated than playing with dolls; algebra is more complicated than single-digit
addition; and *War and Peace* places far more demands on the reader than *Pat
the Bunny.* You have to have a brain that can handle this increased complexity, and the brain changes that occur during adolescence help us get there.

Think of adolescence as a jolt to the system, or, more precisely, two jolts,
one physical and one chemical. The physical jolt is due to the rapid growth of
new connections. So many synaptic connections grow so fast that for a time,
the brain doesn't work as well as it should.

Too many synapses result in a temporary decline in some skills (like the
ability to identify accurately the emotions in the facial expressions of others). Pruning will eliminate the connections that the brain doesn't use. What
remains is a more efficient brain that is better equipped to deal with the additional demands of adulthood.

The second jolt is a chemical one. With the onset of puberty, there is a
rapid production and distribution of new brain chemicals. Puberty is generally associated with reproductive capacity, hence we generally think of
sex hormones, but they are far from being the only story. Numerous other
chemicals first appear during adolescence and, as with an overproduction of
synapses, the brain overproduces some of these chemicals.

This overproduction of synapses and neurotransmitters is probably nature's
way of making sure that enough are produced. In the case of neurotransmitters, the brain produces an abundance of receptor sites. As a result, certain
responses are hyperreactive, and some are the opposite of what they will be
after this transition.

But the overproduction of synapses and of neurochemicals provide only a
partial explanation of the rapid mood swings, the irritability, the risk-taking,
and the poor impulse control that characterize adolescence. To complete this
explanatory picture, it is absolutely essential to include a discussion of the
brain's frontal lobes. The human brain matures from the back to the front; this
explains why sensory functions, such as vision and hearing, appear before
speaking and walking.

The last part of the brain to mature is the front, called the prefrontal cortex.
As it turns out, the prefrontal cortex (PFC) houses those parts of the brain
that we use to decide what to attend to and what we want to remember. The
PFC is also the part of the brain that is responsible for considering the consequences of our actions and for controlling our impulses. It is the frontal
lobes that provide older adolescents and adults with the capacity to inhibit
their impulses, to consider consequences, to plan, to anticipate, to organize,
to delay gratification, and to work toward a goal.

Because the PFC does not mature fully until our mid-twenties, teenagers are
far less able to curb the intense emotions and the mood swings that other parts

of the brain are producing. Eventually, the brain becomes more efficient and eventually develops the capacity to control the urges of early adolescence. But the process is not an easy one for teens, their parents, or their teachers.

Adolescence is best viewed as a journey in three parts. Part 1 is early adolescence. For females it includes ages eleven to thirteen; for boys, it is twelve to fourteen. Early adolescence is a time of rapid mood swings and intense feelings. This is the first wave of emigration when teens leave home, a time when teens trust and value peers over parents as they struggle against parental restrictions that they see as too restrictive.

It is also a time when teens become self-absorbed, convinced that all eyes are on them and increasingly anxious about their hair, their skin, their shape, their clothes, and whether they are being accepted by peers. During this first post-pubertal phase, a flood of new chemicals push teens to take risks, some of which put them in danger.

Part 2 is middle adolescence. For females, it spans ages thirteen to sixteen; for boys the range is larger, from fourteen to twenty years. It is during middle adolescence that teens really separate from parents. But it is also when the frontal lobes show more evidence of maturation and teens are better able to control the impulses they are still feeling.

Part 3, late adolescence, spans ages seventeen to twenty-five for both sexes. Having left their parents to form their own identity, adolescents begin to return to negotiate a more adult-like relationship with parents. Impulses are under (or nearly under) control and the drives for high-risk and novel activities have abated somewhat since their peak in early and middle adolescence.

So what are adults to do during this journey? The first thing to remember is that virtually all areas of development are affected during early adolescence. There are, of course, the obvious changes in physical appearance. Cognitive abilities also show improvements, including the ability to think abstractly and to tackle complex ideas in literature and advanced concepts in math and science. Partly in response to all these rapid changes and partly because of new hormones, there are changes in their emotional lives, with increased stress and anxiety and bouts of despair and dysphoria.

Three important tips for parents. First, set a good example. If you don't want your kids to drink and drive, then don't drink and drive. You want your kids to be honest, then demonstrate honesty. You want them to be polite, then be polite. You don't want them to use profanity, then stop using profanity.

Second, be absolutely certain that your teenager has your support. Let's face it. Even if a parent's worst fears come true, chances are that you are going to be there to support your child. Remember, the journey is more difficult for them than it is for us. No, it doesn't feel that way, but it is.

Third, ensure their safety. They are going to be reckless and thoughtless and they are going to take risks, even if they are told not to do so. But protect them. If they are afraid to call you for a ride when they have had too much to drink you may be putting them in mortal danger.

Shortly after collecting the stories that appear in this book, we asked the principals if they had any specific suggestions. Here are some of their responses:

- Our students must have respect from us in order for them to respect us.
- We need to teach and demonstrate respect and what appropriate ways to behave are.
- They are going to make mistakes, but it is not the end of the world. Mistakes provide the opportunity to grow and to learn.
- Honesty is invaluable when teens make mistakes. If they can be honest, we can deal with what has just happened much easier.
- Students tend not to tell the truth when they fear their parents' wrath.
- Students who tell the truth quickly and take their consequences often have supportive and calm parents.
- It only takes one adult to make a huge impact on a teen's life.
- If parents would allow their students to take responsibility for their actions, there would be fewer times that the students are in trouble for making bad choices.
- Middle school is the learning ground for making better choices.
- Staying calm at all times will encourage middle schoolers to open up and share their innermost anxieties and worries.
- Sometimes the dog really does eat their homework assignment.
- Even though middle schoolers seem to want to separate from adults, this is a time when adults must continue to exert an influence on them.
- Choices are made during middle school years that can influence their entire lives. We need to be there for them.
- Enjoy their humor. Laugh with them when they make mistakes. Hold high expectations for academics and behavior, but always show them you care.
- Dance with them, if they allow you to dance. Remember, they embarrass easily. Tread softly when they need you to back off.
- Ask their opinion on important family matters. Truly listen to them and compromise when it is appropriate.
- Allow them to become somewhat independent by making some choices themselves, but remember they are not ready to make all of their choices.
- One of a principal's best times occurs when we are having one-on-one chats with a student in distress. It may seem minor to the administrator,

but it is often huge to the student. Being there for them will make an indelible impact on their lives.

- When a parent comes in ranting and raving over a suspension, they are modeling this behavior for their student. Know that the student also has to deal with this same parent when the parent is upset with the student. Feel for the student, knowing that things are probably pretty tough at home.
- Until we are able to openly talk with our students and truly show them we care, they will keep us at arm's length.
- Until we can control our emotions and react calmly, middle schoolers will not talk openly. In order to influence their lives and how they will progress through this tough period in their lives, adults must be there for them, care for them, set high expectations for them, but know they will falter. Don't forget, we faltered during our teen years.
- Teens may not admit it, but they love when their parents spend time talking to them. Have lunch with them at school. Bring them lunch at school from a restaurant.
- Patience, consistency, and perseverance are needed for working with middle school age kids. It's not an overnight process and you can't give up even when you wonder if anything is working. Also, you can't just tell kids what they should do. You have to show them by your own actions.

Perhaps principals, teachers, and even parents should begin by taking some form of the Hippocratic oath: First, do no harm.

Appendix
Developmental Characteristics of
Middle School Students

Intellectual Development:

- Display a wide range of individual intellectual development
- Are in a transition period from concrete thinking to abstract thinking
- Are intensely curious and have a wide range of intellectual pursuits, few of which are sustained
- Prefer active over passive learning experiences
- Prefer interaction with peers during learning activities
- Respond positively to opportunities to participate in real-life situations
- Are often preoccupied with self
- Have a strong need for approval and may be easily discouraged
- Develop an increasingly better understanding of personal abilities
- Are inquisitive about adults, often challenging their authority, and always observing them
- May show disinterest in conventional academic subjects but are intellectually curious about the world and themselves
- Are developing a capacity to understand higher levels of humor

Moral Development:

- Are generally idealistic, desiring to make the world a better place and to become socially useful
- Are in transition from moral reasoning which focuses on "what's in it for me" to that which considers the feelings and rights of others

- Often show compassion for those who are downtrodden or suffering and have special concern for animals and the environmental problems that our world faces
- Are moving from acceptance of adult moral judgments to development of their own personal values; nevertheless, they tend to embrace values consonant with those of their parents
- Rely on parents and significant adults for advice when facing major decisions
- Increasingly assess moral matters in shades of grey as opposed to viewing them in black and white terms characteristic of younger children
- At times are quick to see flaws in others but slow to acknowledge their own faults
- Owing to their lack of experience, are often impatient with the pace of change, underestimating the difficulties in making desired social changes
- Are capable of and value direct experience in participatory democracy
- Greatly need and are influenced by adult role models who will listen to them and affirm their moral consciousness and actions as being trustworthy role models
- Are increasingly aware of and concerned about inconsistencies between values exhibited by adults and the conditions they see in society

Physical Development:
- Experience rapid, irregular physical growth
- Undergo bodily changes that may cause awkward, uncoordinated movements
- Have varying maturity rates, with girls tending to mature one and one-half to two years earlier than boys
- May be at a disadvantage because of varied rates of maturity that may require the understanding of caring adults
- Experience restlessness and fatigue due to hormonal changes
- Need daily physical activity because of increased energy
- Develop sexual awareness that increases as secondary sex characteristics begin to appear
- Are concerned with bodily changes that accompany sexual maturation and changes resulting in an increase in nose size, protruding ears, long arms, and awkward posture
- Prefer junk foods but need good nutrition
- Often lack physical fitness, with poor levels of endurance, strength, and flexibility

- Are physically vulnerable because they may adopt poor health habits or engage in risky experimentation with drugs and sex

Emotional/Psychological Development:

- Experience mood swings, often with peaks of intensity and unpredictability
- Need to release energy, often resulting in sudden, apparently meaningless outbursts of activity
- Seek to become increasingly independent, searching for adult identity and acceptance
- Are increasingly concerned about peer acceptance
- Tend to be self-conscious, lack self-esteem, and be highly sensitive to personal criticism
- Exhibit intense concern about physical growth and maturity as profound physical changes occur
- Increasingly behave in ways associated with their gender as sex-role identification strengthens
- Are concerned with many major societal issues as personal value systems develop
- Believe that personal problems, feelings, and experiences are unique to themselves
- Are psychologically vulnerable, because at no other stage in development are they more likely to encounter so many differences between themselves and others

Social Development:

- Have a strong need to belong to a group, with peer approval becoming more important as adult approval decreases in importance
- In their search for self, model behavior after older, esteemed students or nonparent adults
- May exhibit immature behavior because their social skills frequently lag behind their mental and physical maturity
- Experiment with new slang and behaviors as they search for a social position within their group, often discarding these "new identities" at a later date
- Must adjust to the social acceptance of early-maturing girls and the athletic successes of early-maturing boys, especially if they themselves are maturing at a slower rate

- Are dependent on parental beliefs and values but seek to make their own decisions
- Are often intimidated and frightened by their first middle level school experience because of the large numbers of students and teachers and the size of the building
- Desire recognition for their efforts and achievements
- Like fads, especially those shunned by adults
- Often overreact to ridicule, embarrassment, and rejection
- Are socially vulnerable because, as they develop their beliefs, attitudes, and values, the influence of media and negative experiences with adults and peers may compromise their ideals and values

Source: Characteristics of Young Adolescents.
http://www.etsd.org/ems/endorsement/characteristics.htm.

Notes

1. Gale Encyclopedia of Education. "Middle schools." May 6, 2011. Answers. com. http://www.answers.com/ topic/ middle-school.

2. Encyclopedia of Children's Health. "Adolescence." May 6, 2011. http://www. healthofchildren.com /A/ Adolescence.html.

3. Dahl, R. E. 2004. "Adolescent brain development: a period of vulnerabilities and opportunities." *Annals of the New York Academy of Sciences* 1021, 1–22.

4. Knox, R. 2010. "The teen brain: It's just not grown up yet." *NPR Morning Edition.* March 1. http://www.npr.org/templates/story/story.php?storyId=124119468.

5. Woolfolk, A., and N. E. Perry. 2012. *Child and Adolescent Development.* Boston: Pearson.

6. Ostrow, A. 2010. "Social networking dominates our time spent online." August 2. http://mashable.com/2010/08/02/stats-time-spent-online/.

7. Goodreads. http://www.goodreads.com/author/quotes/275648.Socrates.

8. Kraybill, D. B. 2003. *The Amish: Why They Enchant Us.* Scottsdale, PA: Herald Press.

9. MedlinePlus. "Pica." http://www.nlm.nih.gov/medlineplus/ency/article/001538. htm.

10. Spear, L. 2010. *The Behavioral Neuroscience of Adolescence.* New York: Norton.

11. Ackerman, S. J. 2007. "The adolescent brain—The Dana guide." The Dana Foundation. November. http://www.dana.org/ news/brainhealth/detail.aspx?id=10056.

12. Ackerman, "The adolescent brain."

13. Woolfolk and Perry, *Child and Adolescent Development.*

14. Dahl, "Adolescent brain development."

15. Frontline. 2002. "Inside the teenage brain: Interview with Deborah Yurgelun-Todd." http://www.pbs.org/wgbh/pages/frontline/shows/teenbrain/interviews/todd.html.

16. Dahl, "Adolescent brain development."

17. Gingrich, N. 2008. "Let's end adolescence." *Business Week.* October 30.

About the Authors

Richard Marshall, EdD, PhD is an associate professor of education at the University of South Florida Polytechnic and an adjunct associate professor of child psychiatry in the Department of Psychiatry, University of South Florida College of Medicine. In addition to teaching courses in educational psychology and counseling psychology, he recently founded and codirects the USFP Applied Neuroscience and Cognitive Electrophysiology Lab.

A licensed school psychologist with specialty training in pediatric neuropsychology, Dr. Marshall's areas of expertise include the neurobiological bases of learning and behavior problems, the assessment and treatment of disruptive behavior disorders, and school-based interventions for disruptive students. His publications, workshops, and presentations are aimed at helping parents and teachers gain a better understanding of the neurobiology of emotional, behavioral, and learning problems in children and adolescents. His research focus includes the assessment and treatment of child and adolescent psychopathology, the neurobiology of learning and behavior problems, and the genetic correlates of early onset bipolar disorder.

Dr. Marshall's parent and teacher rating scale (the Pediatric Behavior Rating Scale) was published in August 2008. In addition to numerous workshops, he is a featured speaker at national conferences and has coauthored a book for parents, *Handbook for Raising an Emotionally Healthy Child*.

Sharon Neuman is the principal of Lawton Chiles Middle Academy, an accredited math, science, and technology magnet school. She taught elementary school for eight years before becoming an assistant principal and then a principal. She holds a BA from Southeastern University and an MEd from Rollins College.

She has presented at the Florida Association of School Administrators State Conference, Southern Association of Colleges and Schools Summer Conferences, the National Association of Elementary School Principals National Conference, and the National Association of Secondary School Principals National Conference. She has also written articles for several different publications.

Mrs. Neuman has received the Commissioner's Outstanding Principal award and has been recognized as one of three principals in the state for the Innovative Principal of the Year by the Florida Council of Instructional Technology Leaders. Her school was highlighted in *Electronic Learning* and she led her school in becoming the first middle school in her county to go through the Southern Association of Colleges and Schools accreditation process. Her school was one of six schools in the nation highlighted in the National Association of Secondary School Principals (NASSP) decade study on leadership entitled *Leadership for Highly Successful Middle Schools*.

CPSIA information can be obtained at www.ICGtesting.com
Printed in the USA
BVOW070015170312

285319BV00003B/5/P